Geometry

Grades 4–5

by Tiffany Moore

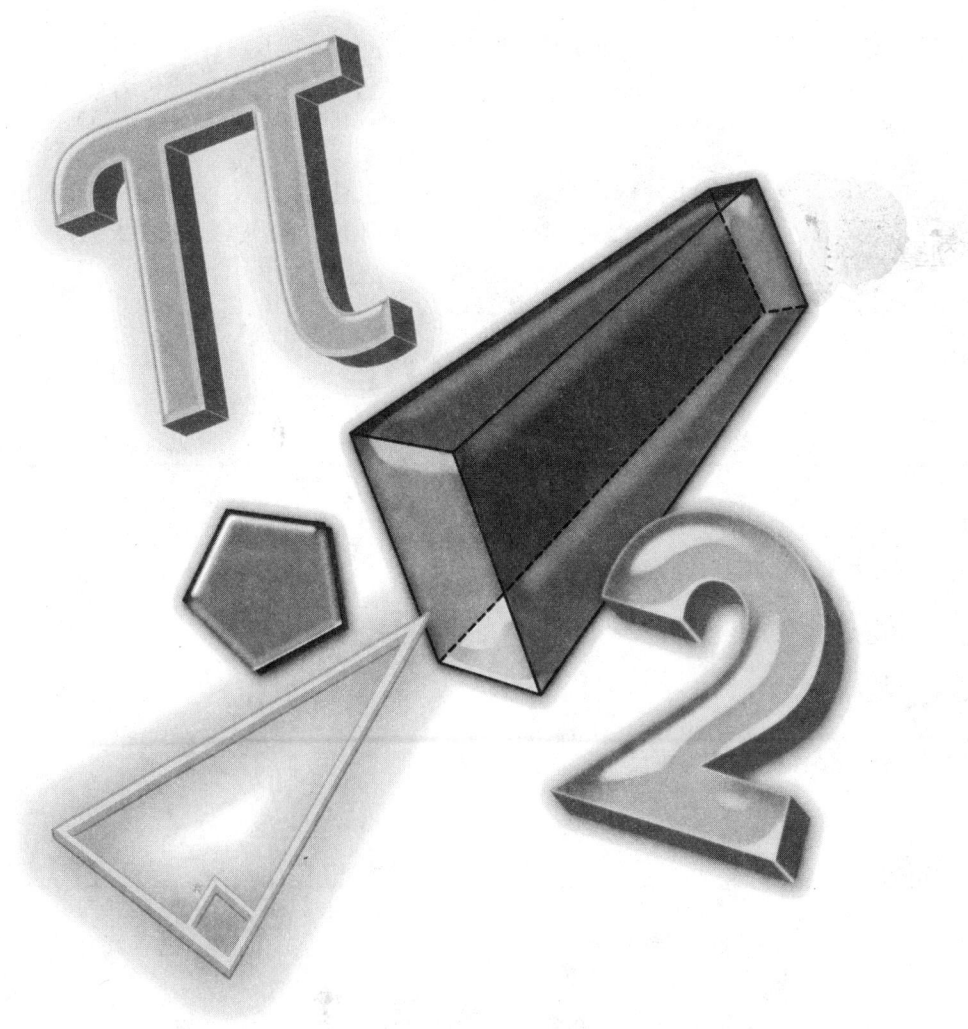

Carson-Dellosa Publishing Company, Inc. • Greensboro, North Carolina

This product has been correlated to state, national, and Canadian provincial standards. Visit *www.carsondellosa.com* to search and view its correlations to your standards.

Credits

Editors: Joey Bland and Barrie Hoople

Inside Illustrations: Lori Jackson and Van Harris

Cover Design: Lori Jackson

Content Review: Jennifer Bonnett

Table of Contents

Table of Contents

Coordinate Graphing

References, Final Review, Answer Key

Introduction

The main objective of *Geometry 4–5* is to give students focused, grade-level appropriate practice to help them develop and reinforce geometry skills. To aid in this experience, the book offers an explanation of each individual skill followed by a variety of activities. These activities will ensure a greater understanding of each skill that is introduced.

Geometry 4–5 is divided into five sections. Each section is designed to lead students through the fundamentals of a skill to a challenging review. The concepts covered in this book include measuring angles; identifying polygons; calculating area, perimeter, and volume; coordinate graphing; and more. Included on page 109 is a list and explanation of common geometric formulas. A glossary of geometric terms is provided on pages 110–113.

Geometry 4–5 is a great way to challenge students and to aid those in need of extra practice. Either focus for this book will yield the same result—an increased interest and understanding of valuable geometric concepts. Observe as your students experience how stimulating geometry can be.

Some Helpful Geometry Symbols

$\longleftrightarrow$ This is the symbol for **line**. It is used above the letters that name a line. For example, $\overleftrightarrow{AB}$ is read **line AB**. Any points on the line may be used to name it.

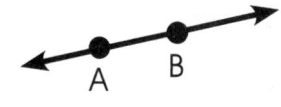

$\longrightarrow$ This is the symbol for **ray**. It is used above the letters that name a ray. For example, $\overrightarrow{CD}$ is read **ray CD**. The endpoint of the ray is written first, and any point on the ray may be used next.

__ This is the symbol for **line segment**. It is used above the letters that name a line segment. For example, $\overline{DE}$ is read **line segment DE**. The line segment must be named by its endpoints.

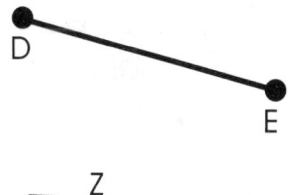

$\angle$ This is the symbol for **angle**. It is used in front of the letters that name an angle. For example, $\angle XYZ$ is read **angle XYZ**. Three points are used to name an angle: an endpoint first, the vertex (middle point) second, and the other endpoint last.

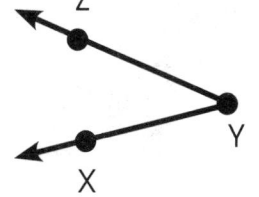

Identifying Points and Lines   Points, Lines, and Angles

A **point** is a position in a plane or in space that has no dimensions.
The points to the right are named Points A, B, and C, or Point A, Point
B, and Point C.

A **line** is a set of points in a straight path that extends infinitely
in two directions. The line to the right is named $\overleftrightarrow{AB}$. Any points
on the line may be used to name it.

Identify the following as a *point*, *points*, or a *line*.

1.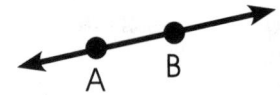

_____

2.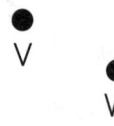

_____

3.

_____

4.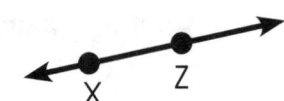

_____

5.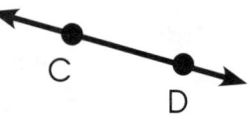

_____

6.

_____

7.

_____

8.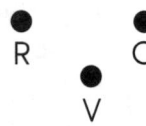

_____

Identifying Rays, Line Segments, and Lines

Points, Lines, and Angles

A **ray** is a portion of a line that extends from one **endpoint** infinitely in one direction. The ray to the right is named $\overrightarrow{AB}$, with the endpoint written first and any point on the ray written next.

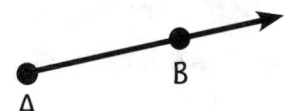

A **line segment** is a finite portion of a line that contains two endpoints. The segment to the right is named $\overline{AB}$. The segment must be named by its two endpoints.

Identify the following as a *line*, *ray*, *line segment*, or *points*.

1.

_____

2.

_____

3.

_____

4.

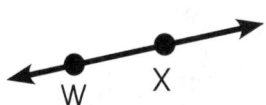

_____

5.

_____

6.

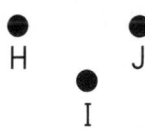

_____

7.

_____

8.

_____

Drawing and Identifying Points, Rays, Line Segments, and Lines

Points, Lines, and Angles

Draw and label each of the following.

1. $\overrightarrow{AB}$

2. Points C and D

3. $\overline{RS}$

4. Points L, M, and N

5. $\overleftrightarrow{MN}$

6. $\overrightarrow{JK}$

Use the figure to the right to answer each question.

7. Name four points. _____

8. Name two line segments. _____

9. Name the line three different ways. _____

10. Name three rays. _____

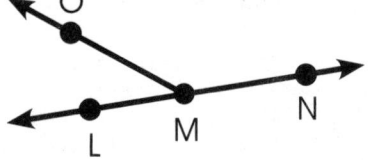

Use the figure to the right to answer each question.

11. Name three points. _____

12. Name the two lines. _____

13. Name four line segments. _____

14. Name four rays. _____

Identifying Intersecting, Perpendicular, and Parallel Lines

Points, Lines, and Angles

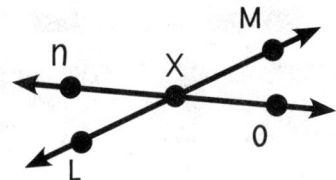

Intersecting lines are lines that cross each other at one point, called the **point of intersection**. X is the point of intersection of lines LM and nO.

Perpendicular lines are two lines that form a right angle at the point of intersection. A small box is used to show that an angle is a right angle (90°).

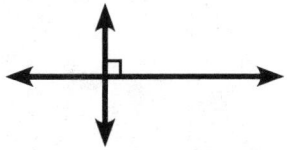

Parallel lines are two lines in the same plane that do not intersect. Small arrows are used to show that lines are parallel.

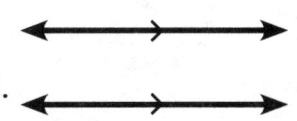

Solve.

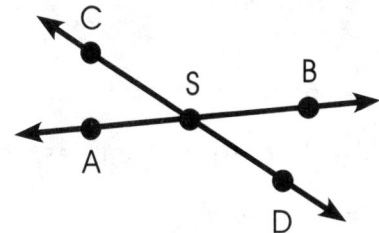

1. What is the point of intersection of $\overleftrightarrow{AB}$ and $\overleftrightarrow{CD}$?

   _____

Draw and label.

2. $\overleftrightarrow{LN}$ intersects $\overleftrightarrow{MK}$ at point B.

3. Y is the point at which $\overleftrightarrow{XZ}$ intersects $\overleftrightarrow{WV}$.

Identify the lines as *parallel*, *perpendicular*, or *neither*.

4.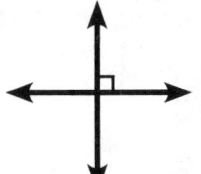

5.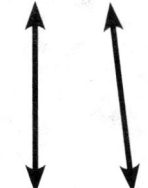

6.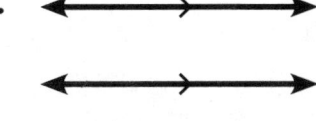

_____   _____   _____

Lines: Mixed Practice

Points, Lines, and Angles

Circle the correct name for each figure.

1. T━━━━━━U   line segment T   line segment TU   line TU

2. X━━━━━━Y   line segment XY   line Y   line XY

3. N━━━━━━M   line segment MN   line M   ray MN

4. R━━━━━━P   line R   line segment RP   line RP

5. B━━━━━━A   line AB   line segment BA   line CA

6. F━━━━━━G   line segment FG   line GF   ray FG

7. C━━━━━━E   line CD   line segment CE   ray CE

8. M━━━━━━N   line segment MN   ray NM   line MN

Circle the correct set of lines.

9. Which lines are perpendicular?

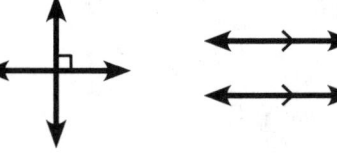

10. Which lines intersect?

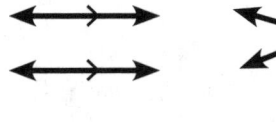

11. Which lines are parallel?

  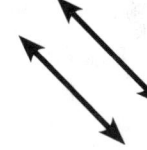

Use the figure to the right to answer each question.

12. Name the point of intersection. _____

13. Name the two lines that intersect. _____

14. Name four line segments. _____

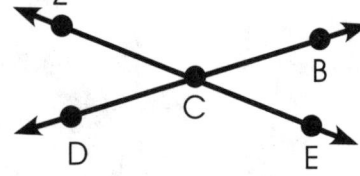

15. Name four rays. _____

Name: _____ Date: _____

Identifying Angles

An **angle** is formed when two rays share an endpoint.

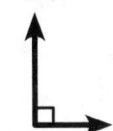

A **right angle** is an angle that measures 90 degrees.

An **obtuse angle** is an angle that measures more than 90 degrees but less than 180 degrees.

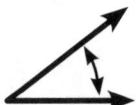

An **acute angle** is an angle that measures less than 90 degrees.

Identify each angle as *right*, *obtuse*, or *acute*.

1.

_____

2.

_____

3.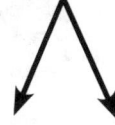

_____

4.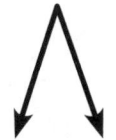

_____

5.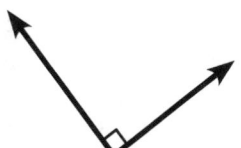

_____

6.

_____

7.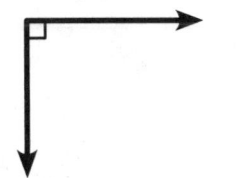

_____

8.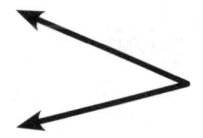

_____

9.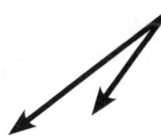

_____

10.

_____

11.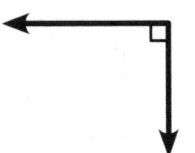

_____

12.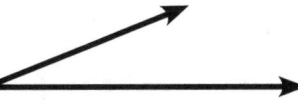

_____

Name: _____   Date: _____

Draw the following angles.

1. right angle

2. obtuse angle

3. acute angle

Below are examples of things you may find around your home. Look at each bolded angle and identify it as *right*, *obtuse*, or *acute*.

4.

_____

5.

_____

6.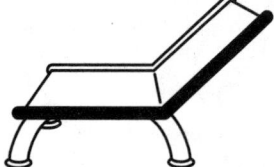

_____

7.

_____

8.

_____

9.

_____

10.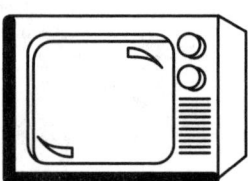

_____

11.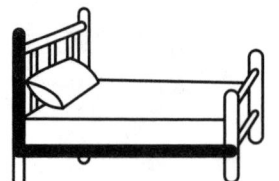

_____

12.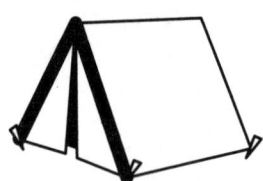

_____

13.

_____

14.

_____

15.

_____

Name: _____   Date: _____

Measuring Angles   Points, Lines, and Angles

Using a protractor will help you draw and measure angles accurately.

How to Use a Protractor

1. Find the center dot or intersecting segments along the straight edge on the bottom of the protractor.

2. Place the dot or intersecting segments over the **vertex**, or point, of the angle you wish to measure.

3. Rotate the protractor so that the zero mark on the straight edge lines up with one side of the angle.

4. Determine which set of numbers you will use. Find the point where the second side of the angle intersects the numbered edge of the protractor. If the angle does not extend far enough to intersect the lines, use the protractor like a ruler to extend the angle line.

5. Read the number that is written on the protractor at the point of intersection. This is the measure of the angle in degrees.

Use a protractor to measure the angle to the nearest degree. Write the number of degrees and the type of angle (*right*, *obtuse*, or *acute*).

1.

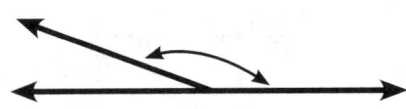

Degrees _____ Type _____

2.

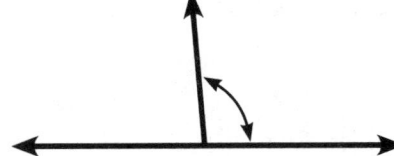

Degrees _____ Type _____

3.

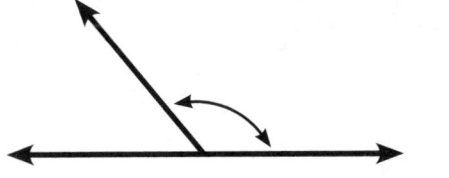

Degrees _____ Type _____

4.

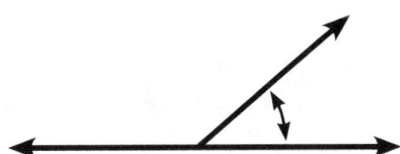

Degrees _____ Type _____

5.

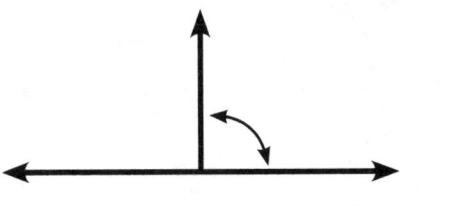

Degrees _____ Type _____

6.

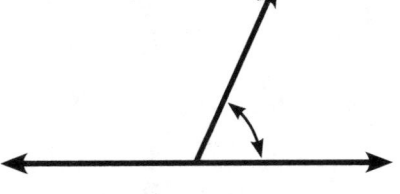

Degrees _____ Type _____

Identifying Planes

Points, Lines, and Angles

A **plane** is a flat surface that extends infinitely in all directions.

Three **noncollinear** points (points not on the same line) are contained in one and only one plane. (You need three points to determine a plane.)

A plane is named using 1–4 points.

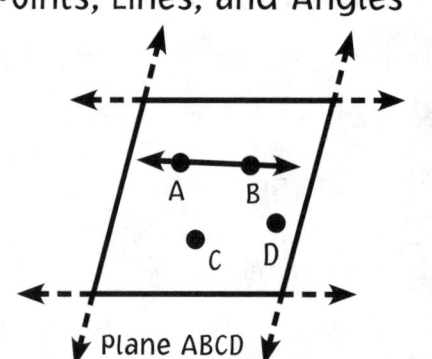

Plane ABCD

---

1. Circle each illustration below that shows a plane.

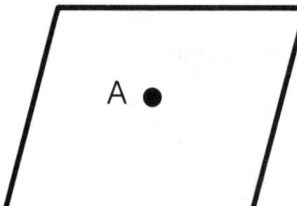 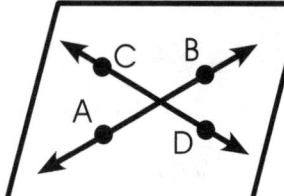 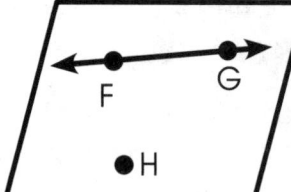 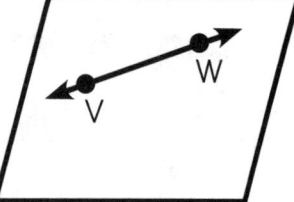

2. Explain why the figure to the right is a plane.

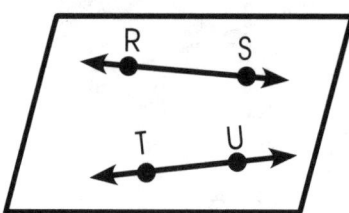

_____

_____

_____

3. Draw plane STUV intersected by $\overleftrightarrow{FG}$ and $\overleftrightarrow{MN}$.

Angles and Lines: Mixed Practice

Points, Lines, and Angles

Use the diagram to solve each problem.

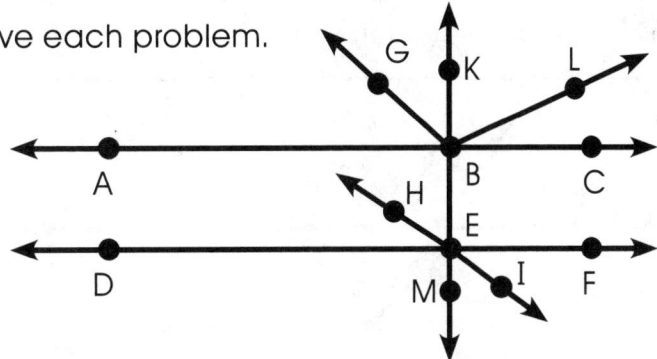

1. Name a pair of parallel lines. _____

2. Name three acute angles. _____

3. Name all of the right angles. _____

4. Name all of the obtuse angles. _____

5. ∠ABG is a (an) _____ angle.

6. ∠EBC is a (an) _____ angle.

7. Line BE is perpendicular to lines _____.

8. Name a pair of intersecting lines. _____

Use the diagram to fill in the answers below.

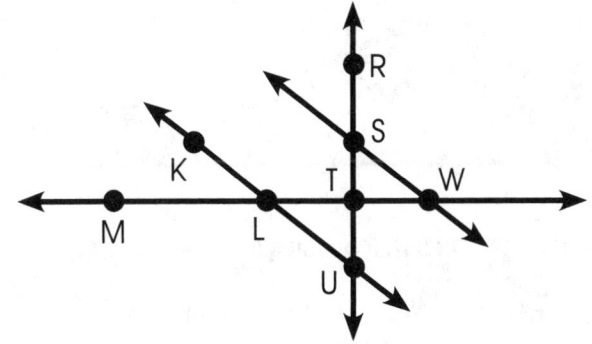

9. Name three points. _____

10. Name two lines. _____

11. Name two perpendicular lines. _____

12. Name two line segments. _____

13. Name two parallel lines. _____

14. Name three rays. _____

Name: _____   Date: _____

Use the diagram to fill in the answers below.

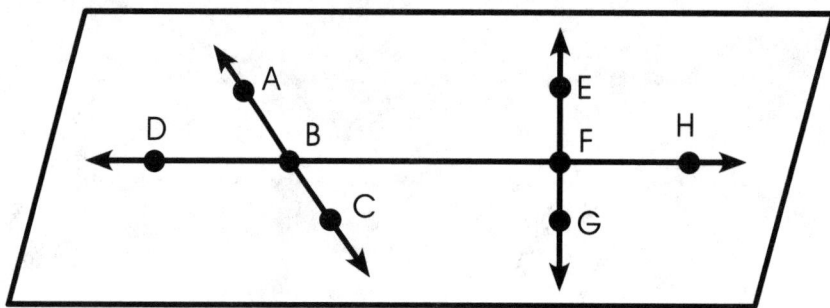

1. Name one point. _____

2. Name five line segments. _____

3. Name each ray. _____

4. Name all of the perpendicular lines. _____

5. Name all of the points on the line DH. _____

6. Name the parallel lines. _____

7. Name a pair of intersecting lines. _____

8. List eight angles. _____

9. Name two intersecting but not perpendicular lines. _____

10. Name the plane. _____

Create a diagram using the following clues.

11. Perpendicular lines AB and CD intersect at point E.

12. ∠AEC and ∠AED are right angles.

13. ∠BEC and ∠BED are right angles.

14. ∠AEF and ∠HEB are obtuse angles.

15. What type of angles are ∠HED and ∠FBE?

Identifying Polygons

A **polygon** is a simple, closed plane figure formed by three or more straight line segments with two sides meeting at each vertex.

1. Which of the following shapes are polygons? _____

A.    B. 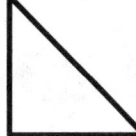   C.

D.    E.    F.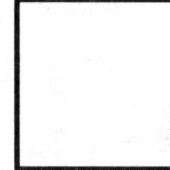

G.    H. 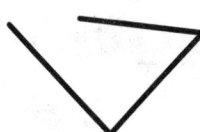   I.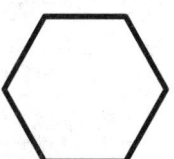

2. Four of the figures above are not polygons. List these figures and explain why they are not polygons.

Figure _____ _____

Figure _____ _____

Figure _____ _____

Figure _____ _____

Name: _____   Date: _____

Naming Polygons   Geometric Figures

Polygons are named for the number of sides they have.

Triangle   **Quadrilateral**   **Pentagon**   **Hexagon**   **Octagon**

____ sides   ____ sides   ____ sides   ____ sides   ____ sides

Complete the table.

Type of Polygon	Number of Sides
1.	3
2. Quadrilateral	
3.	5
4. Hexagon	
5. Heptagon	
6.	8
7. Nonagon	
8. Decagon	

A.

B.

Match figures A–E to the following definitions.

9. _____   a polygon with five sides

C.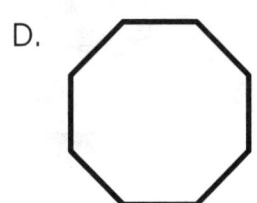

10. _____   a polygon with eight sides

11. _____   a quadrilateral with opposite sides parallel

D.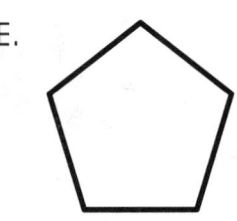

12. _____   a polygon with three angles

E.

13. _____   a polygon with six sides

Classifying Triangles by Sides

Geometric Figures

A **triangle** is a three-sided polygon. A triangle's sides can be used to classify it.

Equilateral Triangle	**Isosceles Triangle**	**Scalene Triangle**
	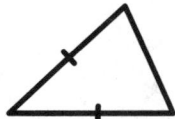	
three congruent sides	two congruent sides	no congruent sides

Line segments that are the same length are said to be **congruent**. Small lines are used to show that line segments are congruent.

Classify each triangle below by its sides. Write *equilateral*, *isosceles*, or *scalene*.

1.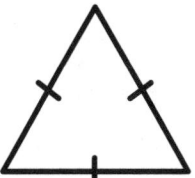

_____

2.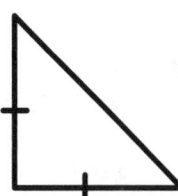

_____

3.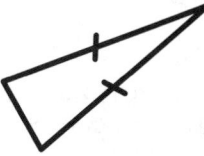

_____

4.

_____

5.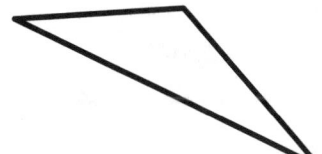

_____

6.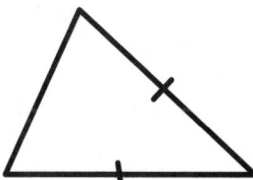

_____

7.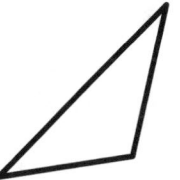

_____

8.

_____

9.

_____

Identifying Triangles by Sides   Geometric Figures

Draw lines to correctly match the terms to their shapes and definitions.

1. equilateral triangle  a triangle that has no congruent sides

2. scalene triangle  a triangle that has three congruent sides

3. isosceles triangle  a triangle that has only two congruent sides

Classify each triangle by the measurements given as *equilateral* triangle, *scalene* triangle, or *isosceles* triangle. Draw and identify each triangle.

56 cm, 40 cm, 56 cm   9 yd., 9 yd., 9 yd.   19 mm, 18 mm, 5 mm

4. _____   **5.** _____   **6.** _____

Draw the following triangles.

7. equilateral triangle   **8.** scalene triangle   **9.** isosceles triangle

Classifying Triangles by Angles

Geometric Figures

A **triangle** is a three-sided polygon. A triangle's angles can be used to classify it.

Acute Triangle	**Equiangular Triangle**	**Right Triangle**	**Obtuse Triangle**
	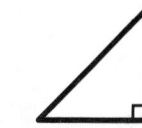		
three acute angles	three congruent angles	one right angle	one obtuse angle

Classify each triangle below by its angles. Write *acute*, *equiangular*, *right*, or *obtuse*.

1.

_____

2.

_____

3.

_____

4.

_____

5.

_____

6.

_____

7.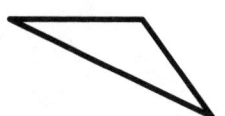

_____

8.

_____

9.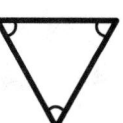

_____

Name: _____ Date: _____

The sum of the three angles of every triangle equals 180°.

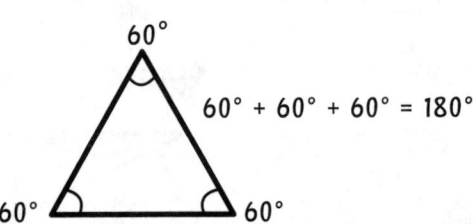 60° + 60° + 60° = 180°

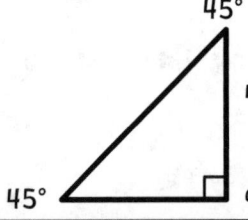 45° + 45° + 90° = 180°

Below are sets of three angles from various types of triangles. Match each set of angles to the most appropriate term.

1. angles 60°, 60°, 60° _____
2. angles 30°, 60°, 90° _____
3. angles 89°, 56°, 35° _____
4. angles 40°, 40°, 100° _____
5. angles 30°, 50°, 100° _____
6. angles 90°, 45°, 45° _____

A. acute

B. obtuse

C. right

D. equiangular

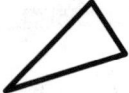

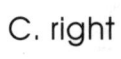
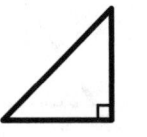
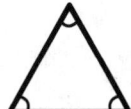

Circle T for True or F for False.

7. A triangle with angles of 110°, 30°, and 40° is obtuse.   T   F
8. A triangle with angles of 60°, 40°, and 80° is right.   T   F
9. A triangle with angles of 60°, 60°, and 60° is equiangular.   T   F
10. A triangle with angles of 70°, 50°, and 60° is acute.   T   F

Explain why each shape below is not possible.

11. Right obtuse triangle _____

_____

_____

12. Triangle with two obtuse angles _____

_____

_____

Classifying Triangles: Mixed Practice Geometric Figures

Circle the appropriate term for each triangle.

1.    right   obtuse   acute

2.    isosceles   equilateral   scalene

3.    isosceles   equilateral   scalene

4.    isosceles   equilateral   scalene

5.    equiangular   obtuse   acute

6.    isosceles   equilateral   scalene

7. 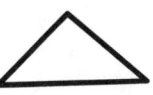   scalene   equilateral   isosceles

8.    right   acute   equilateral

9. 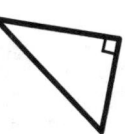   acute   obtuse   right

10.    isosceles   equilateral   scalene

11.    isosceles   equilateral   scalene

12. 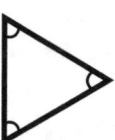   obtuse   equiangular   right

Name: _____ Date: _____

Match each description with the correct triangle name from the box.

1. Side lengths are 3 cm, 4 cm, 5 cm. _____

2. Angles measure 30°, 60°, 90°. _____

3. Angles measure 25°, 10°, 145°. _____

4. Side lengths are 7 ft., 6 ft., 7 ft. _____

5. Side lengths are 7 in., 7 in., 7 in. _____

6. Angles measure 60°, 60°, 60°. _____

7. Angles measure 50°, 88°, 42°. _____

| A. right |
| B. obtuse |
| C. acute |
| D. equiangular |
| E. scalene |
| F. equilateral |
| G. isosceles |

Complete each statement using *sometimes*, *always*, or *never*.

8. An obtuse triangle is _____ an isosceles triangle.

9. A triangle _____ has a right angle and an obtuse angle.

10. An isosceles triangle is _____ an equilateral triangle.

Circle the correct triangle name below each description.

11. A triangle with two 45° angles

   A. right   B. acute   C. equiangular   D. obtuse   E. scalene

12. A triangle made up of angles that all measure 60°

   A. right   B. acute   C. equiangular   D. obtuse   E. scalene

Angle Measurements in a Triangle   Geometric Figures

The sum of all angles of a triangle is 180°. Use that information to find the unknown angle for each triangle. Use the space at the right to show your work.

1.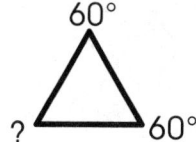

_____

2.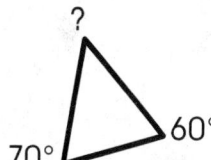

_____

3.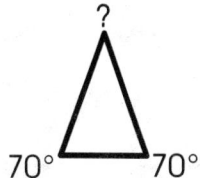

_____

4.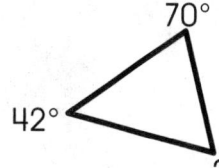

_____

5.

_____

6.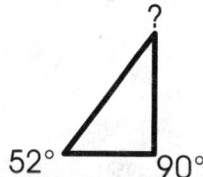

_____

7.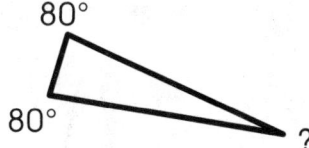

_____

8.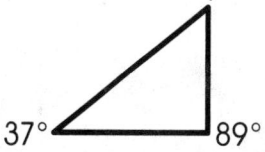

_____

Unknown Angles

Find the unknown angle in each triangle.

1.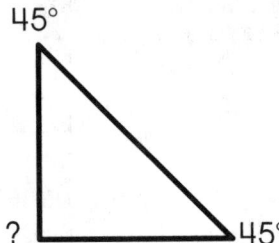

2.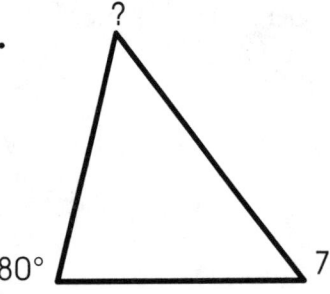

3.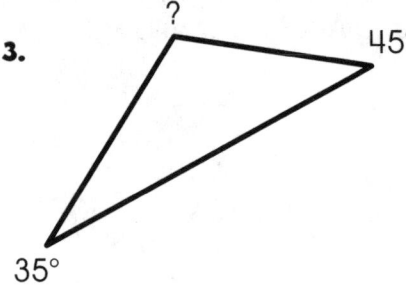

4.

5.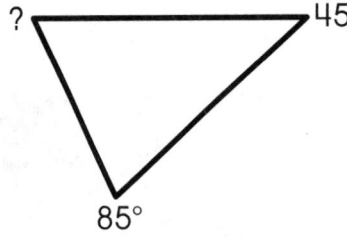

6.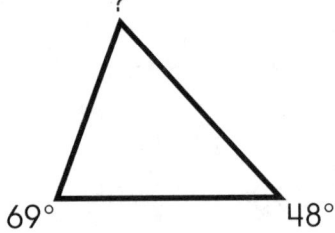

7.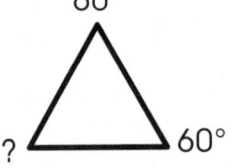

8.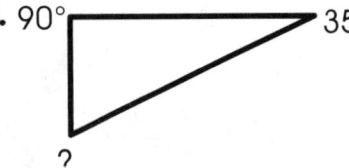

9.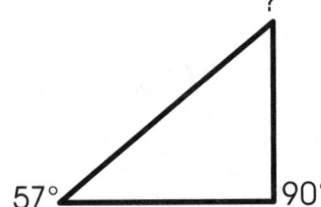

10.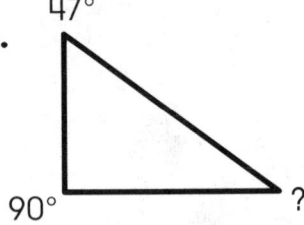

11.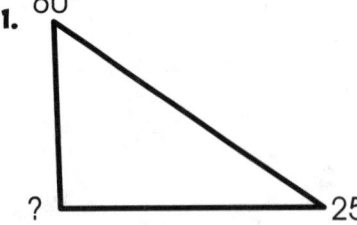

12.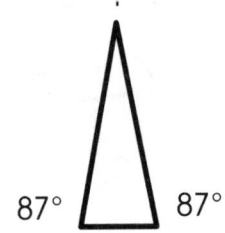

Quadrilaterals: Parallelograms and Trapezoids

Geometric Figures

A **parallelogram** is a quadrilateral with opposite sides parallel. Opposite sides and angles are congruent.

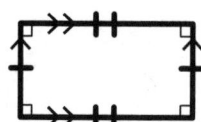 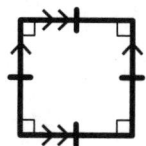 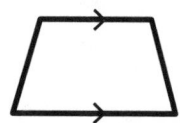 

A **rectangle** is a parallelogram with four right angles. Opposite sides are congruent and parallel.

A **square** is a rectangle with congruent sides. Opposite sides are parallel.

A **trapezoid** is a quadrilateral with exactly one pair of parallel sides.

A **rhombus** is a parallelogram with four congruent sides. Opposite angles are congruent and opposite sides are parallel.

Name each figure.

1.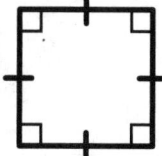

_____

2.

_____

3.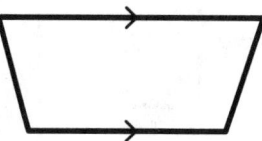

_____

4.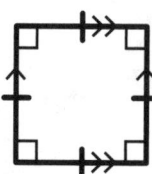

_____

5.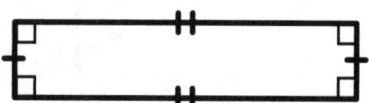

_____

6.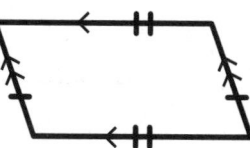

_____

7.

_____

8.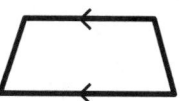

_____

Name: _____   Date: _____

Angle Measurements in Quadrilaterals   Geometric Figures

The sum of the angles in any quadrilateral is 360°.

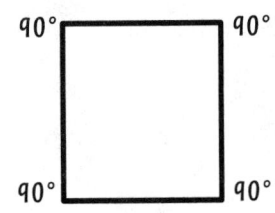

90° + 90° + 90° + 90° = 360°   90° + 90° + 140° + 40° = 360°

Find the unknown angle for each quadrilateral.

1.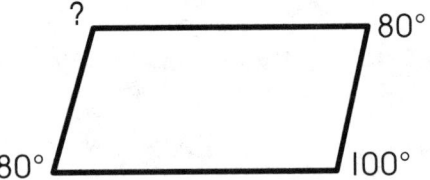

2.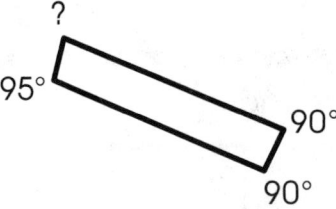

3.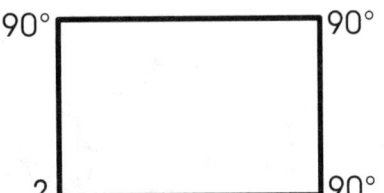

4.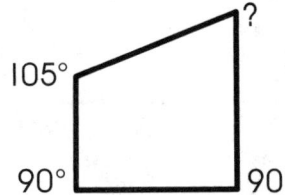

5.

6.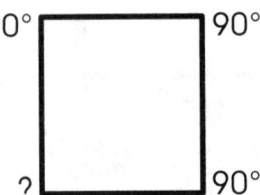

7.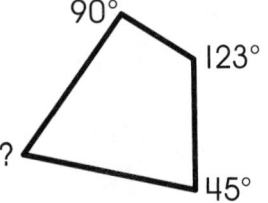

8.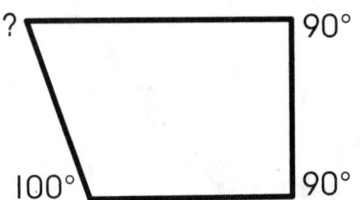

Other Polygons

Geometric Figures

A **pentagon** is a polygon with five sides. A regular pentagon has five congruent sides and five congruent angles.

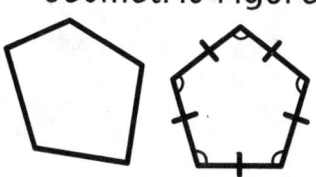

A **hexagon** is a polygon with six sides. A regular hexagon has six congruent sides and six congruent angles.

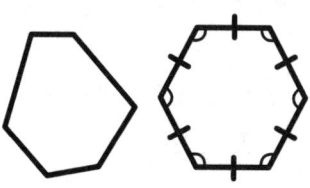

An **octagon** is a polygon with eight sides. A regular octagon has eight congruent sides and eight congruent angles.

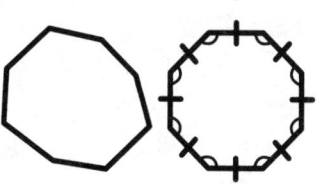

Name the figure and write *R* for regular or *I* for irregular.

1.

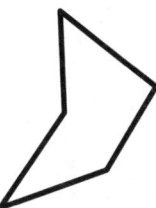

_____

2.

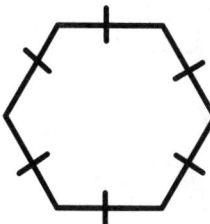

_____

3.

_____

4.

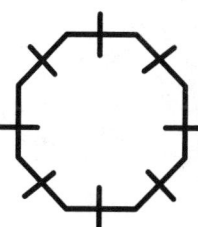

_____

5.

_____

6.

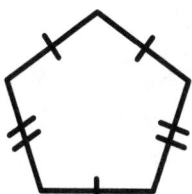

_____

Name: _____ Date: _____

Identify each figure by writing its name and a brief description of the figure.

	Name	**Description**

1.  _____ _____

2. 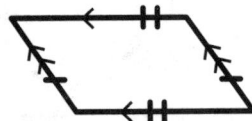 _____ _____

3. 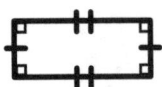 _____ _____

4. 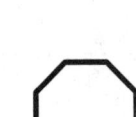 _____ _____

5.  _____ _____

6.  _____ _____

7. _____ _____

8. _____ _____

Polygon Puzzle

Geometric Figures

Read the list of definitions for geometric figures. Match the definitions with the appropriate figures to solve the puzzle below.

I. a polygon with six sides

M. a quadrilateral with opposite sides parallel—opposite angles are congruent but are not necessarily right angles

T. a plane figure with four equal sides and four right angles—opposite sides are parallel

F. a quadrilateral with four right angles—opposite sides are parallel, but not all sides are equal

E. a quadrilateral with two nonparallel sides and two parallel sides

A. an obtuse triangle

G. an irregular polygon

O. a polygon with three acute angles

S. a polygon with five sides

Y. a polygon with eight sides

R. has no angles or sides

Name: _____   Date: _____

Section A. Draw a line to match the name of each polygon to its definition.

1. pentagon

2. parallelogram

3. square

4. hexagon

5. rectangle

6. octagon

7. triangle

8. trapezoid

9. quadrilateral

10. polygon

A. a polygon with six sides

B. a quadrilateral with opposite sides that are parallel and congruent

C. a polygon with three angles

D. a plane figure in which all angles are right angles—opposite sides are parallel and congruent

E. a rectangle with all four sides congruent—opposite sides are parallel, and opposite angles are congruent

F. a polygon with five sides

G. three or more line segments connected so that the area is closed in

H. a polygon with eight sides

I. any figure with four sides

J. a quadrilateral with two nonparallel sides and two parallel sides

Section B. Draw each figure on the dot grid.

11. Draw a triangle.

12. Draw a pentagon.

13. Draw a quadrilateral.

14. Draw an octagon.

15. Draw a trapezoid.

16. Draw a hexagon.

Identifying Parts of a Circle

A **circle** is a closed curve with all points in one plane and equidistant from a fixed point (the center).

This circle is circle G.

The **radius** is $\overline{CG}$.

The **diameter** is $\overline{CD}$.

$\overline{AB}$, $\overline{CD}$, and $\overline{EF}$ are **chords**.

The **center** is G.

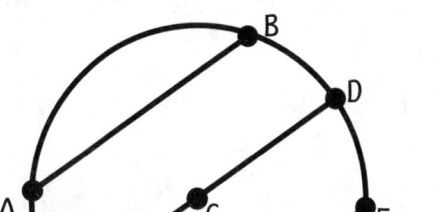

Identify the parts of each circle. Write one answer for each part.

Circle M

1. radius _____

2. chord _____

3. diameter _____

4. center _____

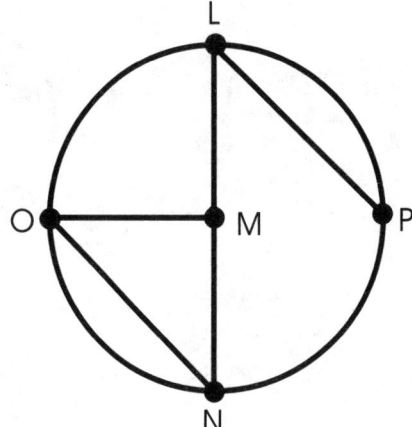

Circle R

5. radius _____

6. chord _____

7. diameter _____

8. center _____

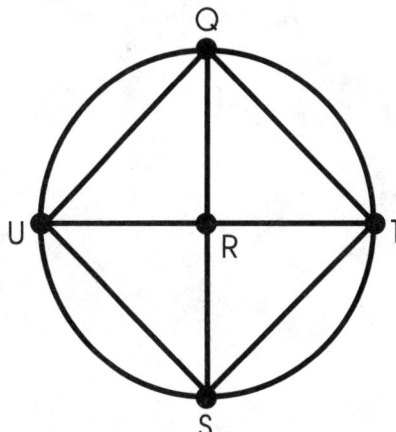

Name: _____   Date: _____

Finding the Diameter of a Circle   Geometric Figures

The **diameter** of a circle is a line segment that joins two points on a circle and passes through the center.

The **radius** is the line segment, or distance, from the center of a circle to a point on the circle.

What is the diameter of circle B?

d = diameter and r = radius

d = 2r

d = 2(15 m)

d = 30 m

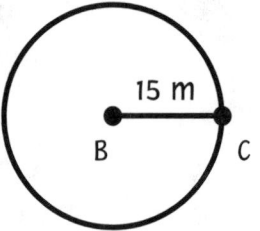

Find the diameter of each circle.

1. (12 cm)

2.  (62 ft.)

3. 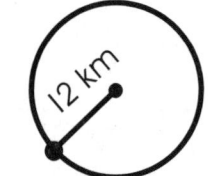 (12 km)

4. 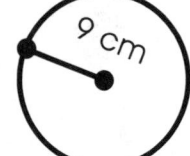 (9 cm)

_____   _____   _____   _____

5. (26 m)

6.  (84 in.)

7.  (33 in.)

8.  (112 ft.)

_____   _____   _____   _____

Finding the Radius of a Circle
Geometric Figures

The **radius** is the line segment, or distance, from the center of a circle to a point on the circle.

The **diameter** of a circle is a line segment that joins two points on a circle and passes through the center.

What is the radius of circle F?

r = radius and d = diameter

r = d/2

r = 26 cm/2

r = 13 cm

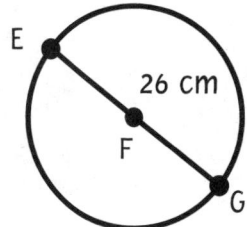

Find the radius of each circle.

1. 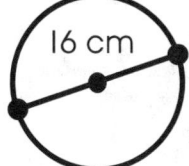 16 cm

_____

2. 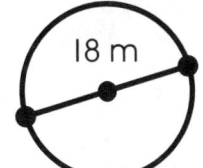 18 m

_____

3.  14 ft.

_____

4. 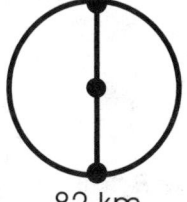 82 km

_____

5. 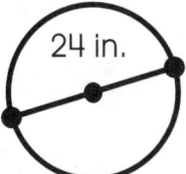 24 in.

_____

6. 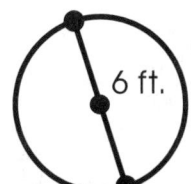 6 ft.

_____

7. 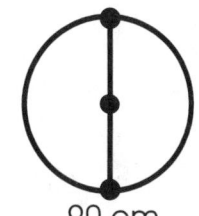 90 cm

_____

8.  48 yd.

_____

Diameter and Radius: Mixed Practice   Geometric Figures

The radius is half the diameter of a circle. To find the diameter, double the radius.

What is the diameter of the circle?

d = 2(8 cm)

d = 16 cm

The diameter is 16 cm.

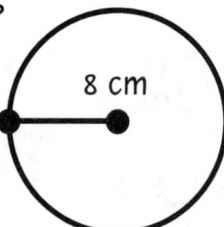

8 cm

Use the radius to find the diameter. Show your work.

1. Radius is 39 in.

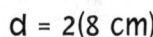

_____

2. Radius is 9 cm.

_____

3. Radius is 20 cm.

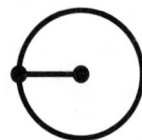

_____

4. Radius is 14 mm.

_____

5. Radius is 6 ft.

_____

6. Radius is 4 yd.

_____

Use the diameter to find the radius. Show your work.

7. Diameter is 12 cm.

_____

8. Diameter is 6 ft.

_____

9. Diameter is 22 yd.

_____

10. Diameter is 10 in.

_____

11. Diameter is 16 in.

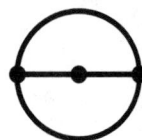

_____

12. Diameter is 4 cm.

_____

Labeling the Parts of a Circle

Geometric Figures

A **center** is the center point of a circle or sphere naming the circle or sphere (center A, circle A).

A **chord** is a line segment passing through a circle that has its endpoints on that circle (chord $\overline{BC}$).

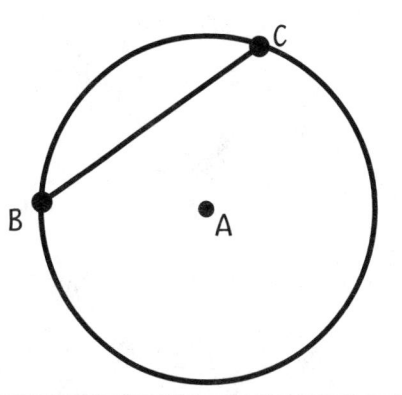

Label the parts on the circle that are listed below.

1. chord $\overline{AD}$
2. center B
3. radius $\overline{BC}$
4. chord $\overline{EC}$
5. diameter $\overline{EG}$
6. radius $\overline{BG}$

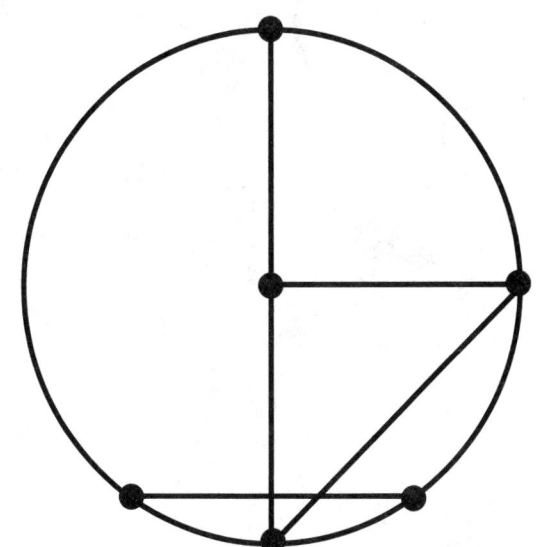

Label the parts on the circle that are listed below.

7. center M
8. radius $\overline{PM}$
9. radius $\overline{MN}$
10. chord $\overline{PQ}$
11. diameter $\overline{LN}$
12. chord $\overline{NO}$

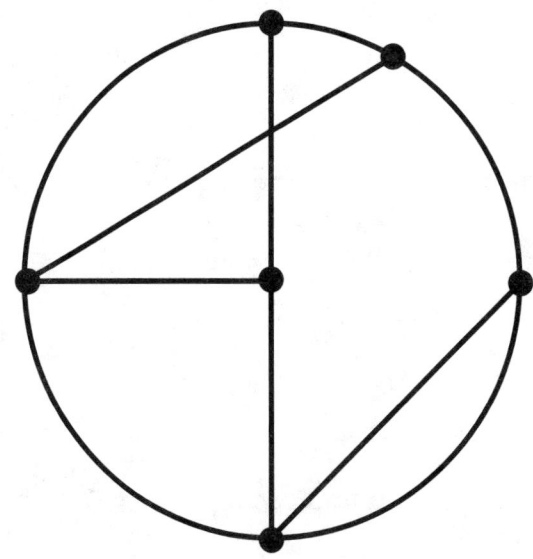

Labeling Circles

Write the names of the parts of the circles below.

1.
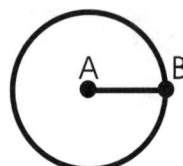

_____

2.
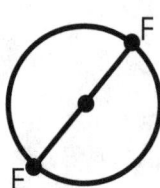

_____

3.

_____

4.
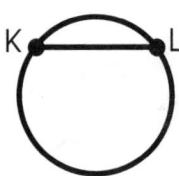

_____

5.
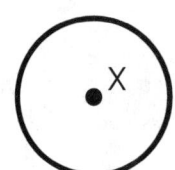

_____

6.
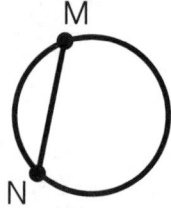

_____

7.

_____

8.
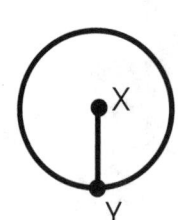

_____

9.
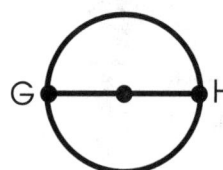

_____

10.
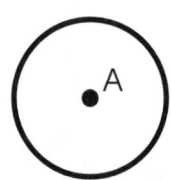

_____

11.
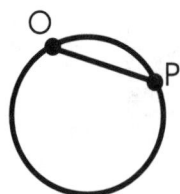

_____

12.

_____

13.

_____

14.
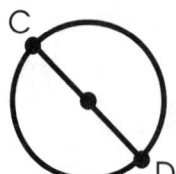

_____

15.
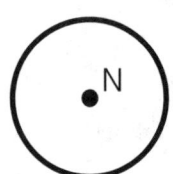

_____

Drawing Circles   Geometric Figures

Draw each circle in the box.

1. Draw circle D, with a diameter $\overline{AB}$, chord $\overline{LM}$, and radius $\overline{DE}$.

2. Draw circle T, with radius $\overline{TN}$, chord $\overline{MN}$, chord $\overline{OP}$, and diameter $\overline{RN}$.

3. Draw circle E, with diameter $\overline{DF}$, radius $\overline{EG}$, and chord $\overline{GF}$.

4. Draw circle B, with chord $\overline{FC}$, chord $\overline{AE}$, diameter $\overline{AC}$, radius $\overline{BE}$, and radius $\overline{BF}$.

Name: _____ Date: _____

Circles: Mixed Practice   Geometric Figures

Circle the answers.

1. The diameter of a circle is:

two times the radius   triple the radius   radius minus radius

2. The radius of a circle is:

diameter squared   two times the diameter   diameter divided by two

Use the figure to the right to circle the correct answers below.

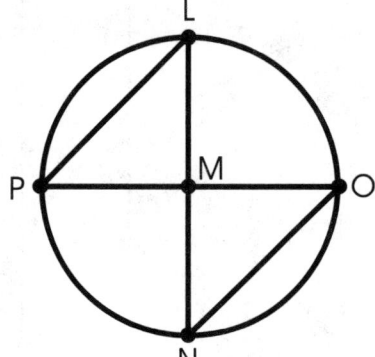

3. $\overline{LN}$ is:

radius   diameter   chord   center

4. $\overline{PO}$ is:

radius   diameter   chord   center

5. $\overline{MO}$ is:

radius   diameter   chord   center

6. Point M is:

radius   diameter   chord   center

7. $\overline{ON}$ is:

radius   diameter   chord   center

8. The length of $\overline{MO}$ is the same as:

$\overline{PL}$ $\overline{PO}$ $\overline{LN}$ $\overline{MN}$

Name: _____ Date: _____

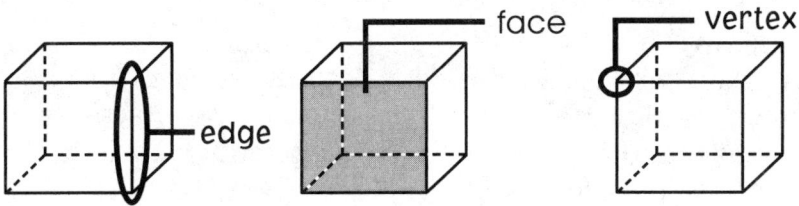
Finish the table.

	Figure	Number of Faces	Number of Edges	Number of Vertices
1.	Triangular Prism			
2.	Rectangular Prism			
3.	Triangular Pyramid			
4.	Cube			
5.	Square Pyramid			

Name: _____ Date: _____

A **prism** is a solid figure in which two faces are polygons in parallel planes and the other faces are parallelograms.

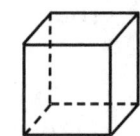

A **cube** is a solid figure in which every face is a square and every edge is the same length.

A **pyramid** is a solid figure in which the base is a polygon and the faces are triangles with a common vertex.

Label each solid figure as *prism*, *cube*, or *pyramid*.

1.

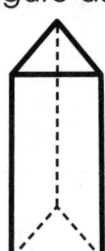

_____

2.

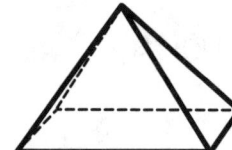

_____

3.

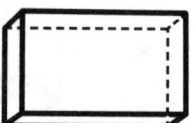

_____

4.

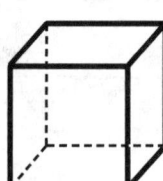

_____

5.

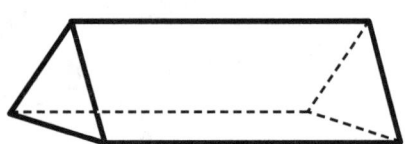

_____

6.

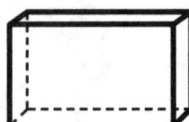

_____

7.

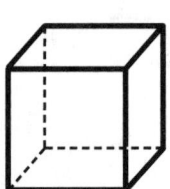

_____

8.

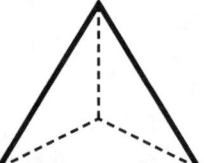

_____

Name: _____ Date: _____

A **cylinder** is a solid figure formed by two congruent parallel circles joined by a curved surface.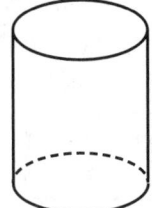

A **cone** is a solid figure with a circular base joined to a vertex by a curved surface.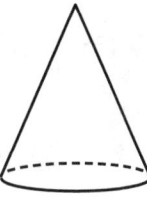

A **sphere** is a solid figure formed by a set of points that are all the same distance from a fixed point called the center.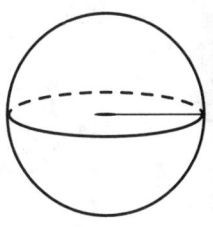

Below are examples of solid figures from the real world. Write *cylinder*, *cone*, or *sphere*.

1.

_____

2.

_____

3.

_____

4.

_____

5.

_____

6.

_____

7.

_____

8.

_____

Challenge: 2-D Nets
Geometric Figures

Think about unfolding a cube-shaped cardboard box. All of the faces would be squares that are attached along the edges. A diagram of this unfolded box is called a **net**.

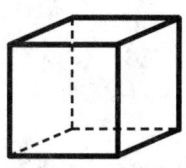 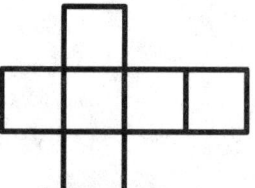

Write the name of the solid figure represented by the following nets.

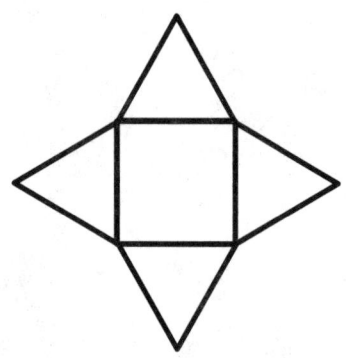

1. _____

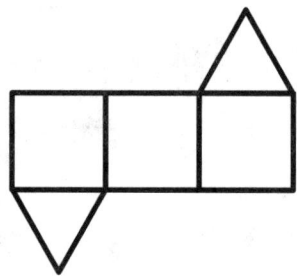

2. _____

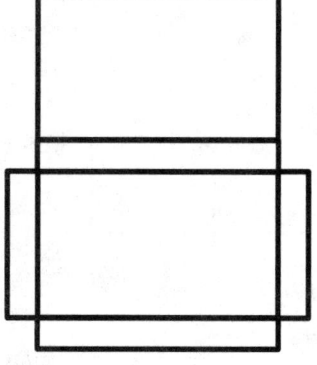

3. _____

Name: _____   Date: _____

Solid Figures: Mixed Practice   Geometric Figures

Name and draw the following solid figures.

Definition	Name	Drawing

1. a solid figure formed by two congruent parallel circles joined by a curved surface

_____

2. a solid figure in which every face is a square and every edge is the same length

_____

3. a prism in which two faces are triangles

_____

4. a solid figure in which all six faces are rectangles with three pairs of parallel, congruent, opposite faces

_____

5. a solid figure formed by a set of points that are all the same distance from a fixed point called the center

_____

6. a solid figure with a circular base joined to a vertex by a curved surface

_____

Which solid figures have the following characteristics?

7. 6 faces, 8 vertices, 12 edges

_____

8. 5 vertices, 8 edges, 5 faces

_____

9. 5 faces, 9 edges, 6 vertices

_____

10. 4 faces, 4 vertices, 6 edges

_____

Name: _____ Date: _____

Drawing Solid Figures

Draw each solid figure described below and write its name. Use the key to help you.

Key					
cone	cylinder	sphere	triangular pyramid	cube	rectangular prism

1. 6 congruent faces, 8 vertices, 12 edges

2. 0 faces, 0 vertices, 0 edges

_____

_____

3. 2 faces, 1 curved surface

4. 6 faces, 12 edges, 8 vertices

_____

_____

5. 1 base, 1 curved surface, 1 vertex

6. 4 vertices, 6 edges, 4 faces

_____

_____

Geometric Figure Sort 1

1. Sort the following plane figures by drawing them in the Venn diagram below.

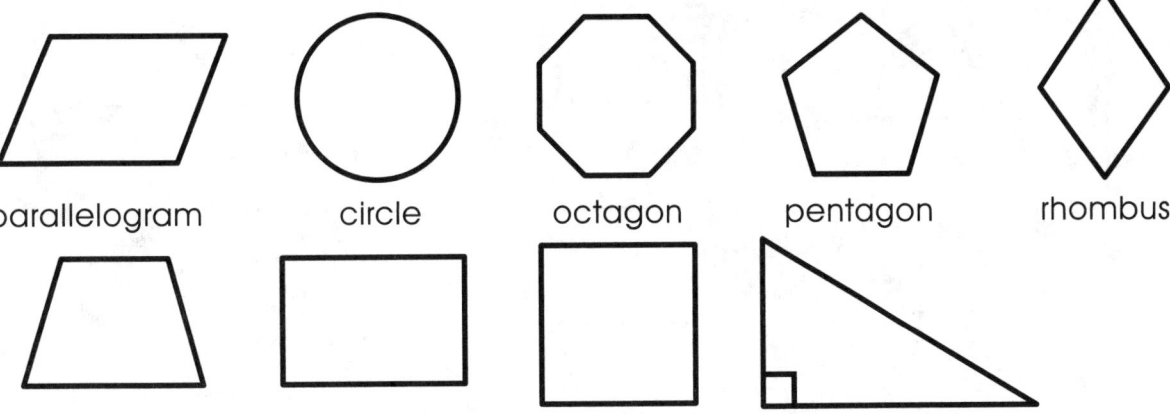

parallelogram   circle   octagon   pentagon   rhombus

trapezoid   rectangle   square   right triangle

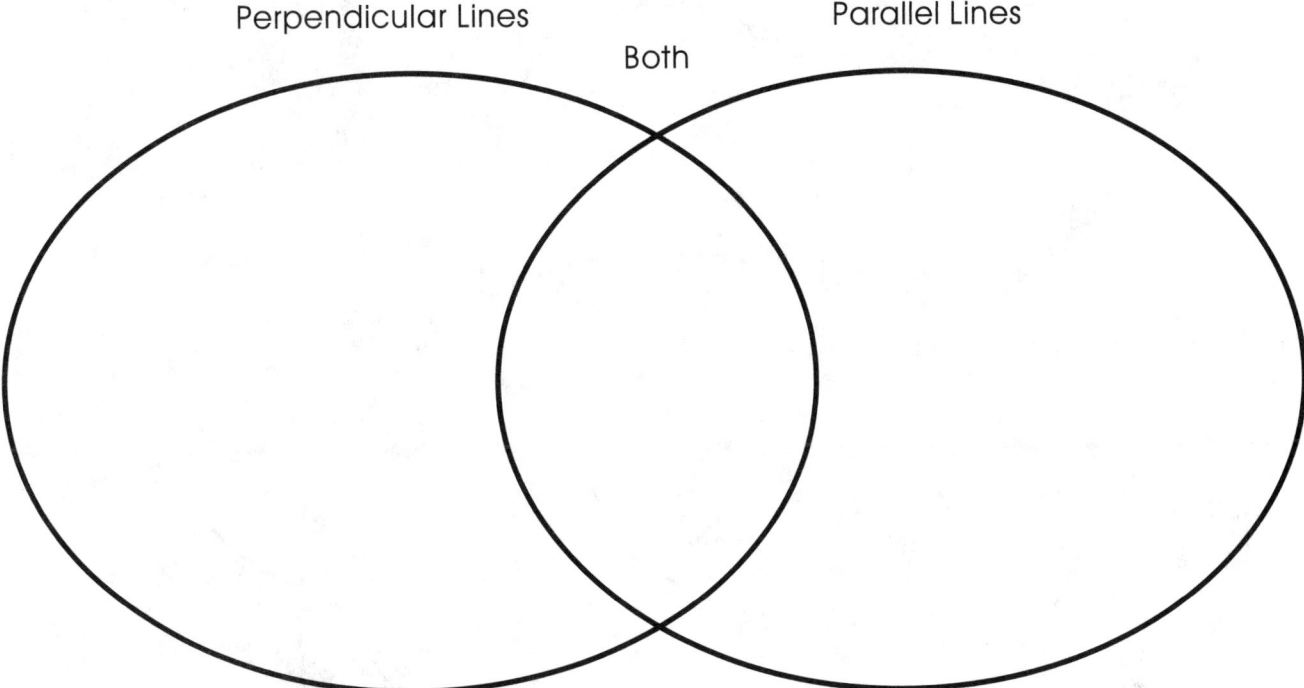

Perpendicular Lines   Parallel Lines

Both

2. Which figures do not fit into the Venn diagram? _____

3. Which figures have both parallel and perpendicular lines? _____

_____

Name: ______________________ Date: ______________

Geometric Figure Sort 2

Geometric Figures

Sort the following figures into the Venn diagram.

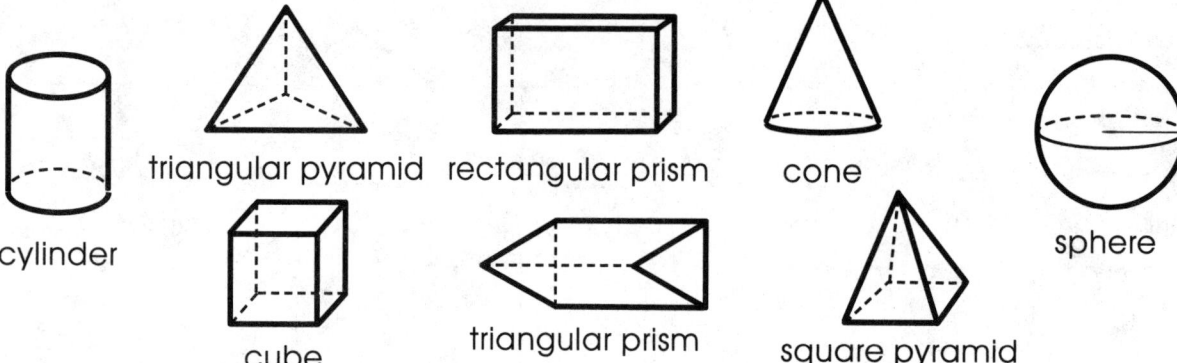

triangular pyramid
rectangular prism
cone
cylinder
sphere
cube
triangular prism
square pyramid

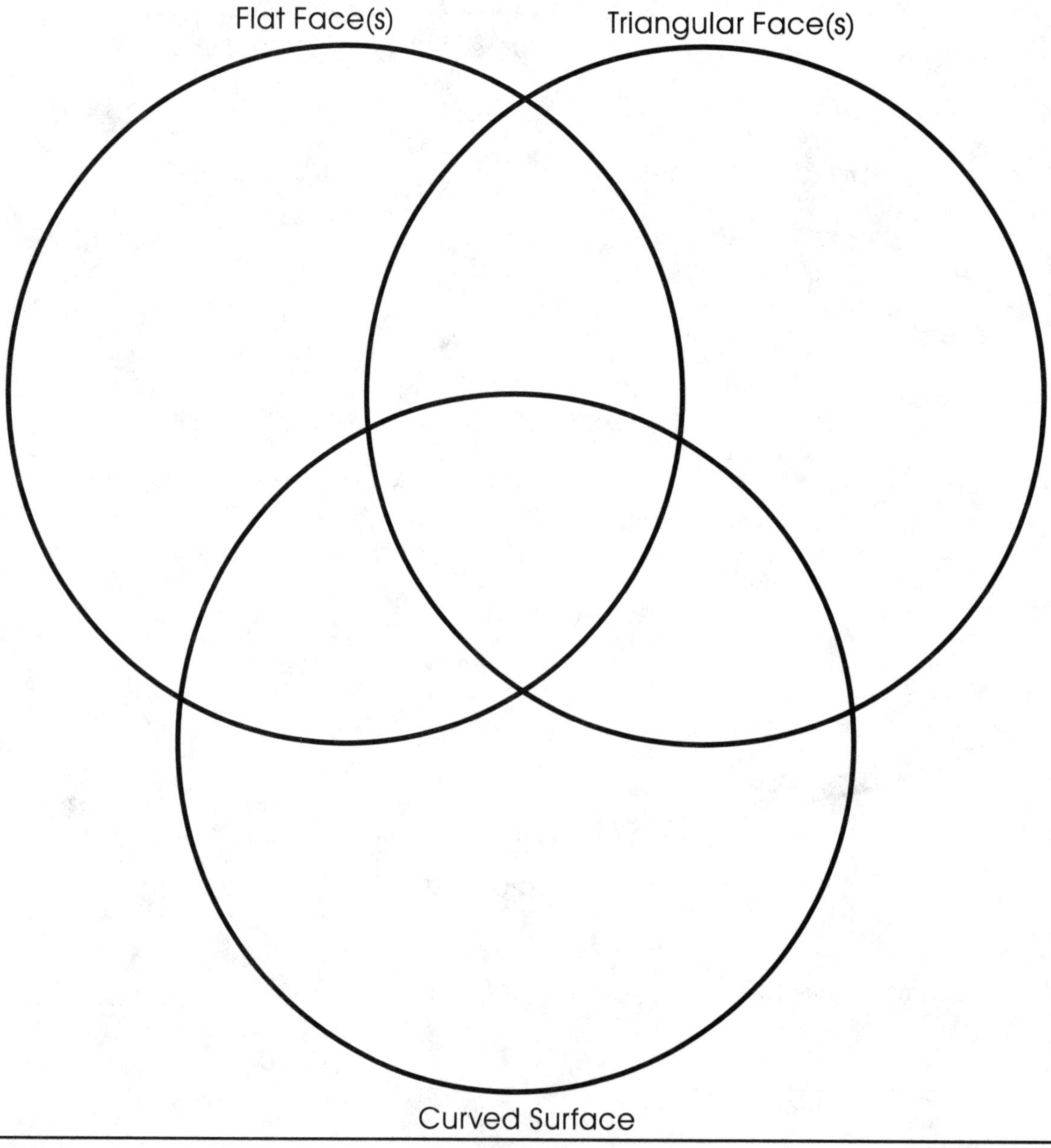

Flat Face(s)
Triangular Face(s)
Curved Surface

Geometric Figures: Mixed Practice

Geometric Figures

Across

1. a polygon with five sides
2. a quadrilateral with four right angles—opposite sides are parallel, but not all sides are congruent
4. a point where three or more faces intersect
6. a polygon with six sides
8. a polygon with eight sides
10. a solid figure in which every face is a square and every edge is the same length
11. a quadrilateral with four right angles—opposite sides are parallel, and all sides are congruent
12. any figure with four sides
13. a solid figure in which all six faces are rectangles with three pairs of opposite faces that are parallel and congruent

Down

1. a quadrilateral with parallel opposite sides
3. a quadrilateral with two nonparallel sides and two parallel sides
5. a line segment where two faces of a solid figure meet
7. a plane figure that serves as one side of a solid figure
9. a solid figure formed by two congruent parallel circles joined by a curved surface
11. a solid figure formed by a set of points that are all the same distance from a fixed point called the center

Perimeter

Area, Perimeter, and Volume

Perimeter is the total distance around a given figure. To find the perimeter, add the lengths of the sides of the figure.

Example: P = perimeter

P = 4 cm + 8 cm + 4 cm + 8 cm

P = 24 cm

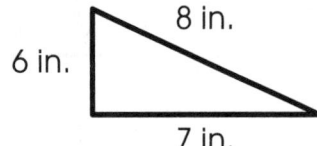

8 cm

4 cm   4 cm

8 cm

Find the perimeter of each figure below by adding the lengths of the sides.

1.
15 yd.
10 yd.   10 yd.
15 yd.

_____

2.
8 in.
6 in.
7 in.

_____

3.
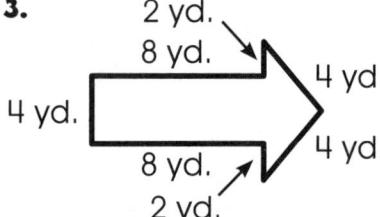
2 yd.
8 yd.
4 yd.   4 yd.
4 yd.
8 yd.
2 yd.

_____

4.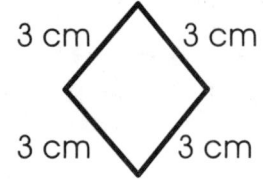
3 cm   3 cm
3 cm   3 cm

_____

5.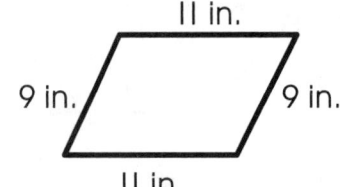
11 in.
9 in.   9 in.
11 in.

_____

6.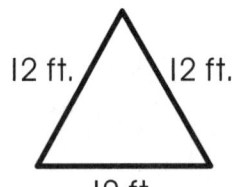
12 ft.   12 ft.
12 ft.

_____

7.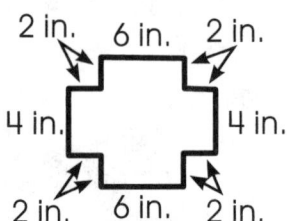
2 in.   6 in.   2 in.
4 in.   4 in.
2 in.   6 in.   2 in.

_____

8.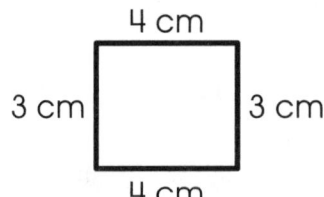
4 cm
3 cm   3 cm
4 cm

_____

9.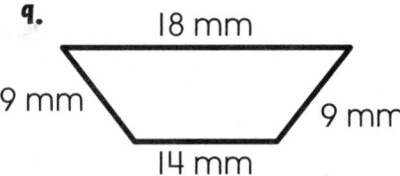
18 mm
9 mm   9 mm
14 mm

_____

10.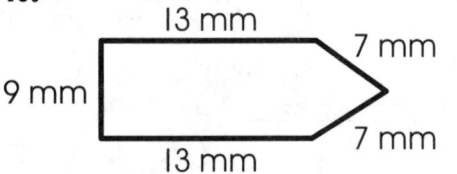
13 mm
7 mm
9 mm
7 mm
13 mm

_____

11.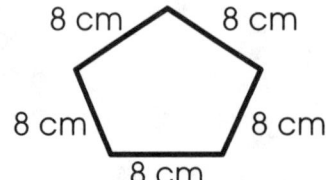
8 cm   8 cm
8 cm   8 cm
8 cm

_____

12.
4 in. 4 in.
5 in.   5 in.
5 in.   5 in.
4 in.   4 in.
5 in.

_____

Name: _____   Date: _____

Perimeter of Polygons   Area, Perimeter, and Volume

Solve for *n* to find the missing side.

1.

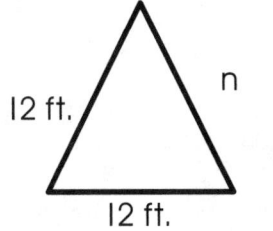

P = 36 ft., n = _____

2.

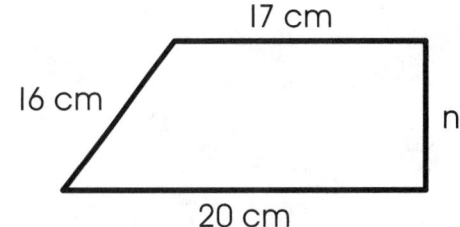

P = 68 cm, n = _____

3.

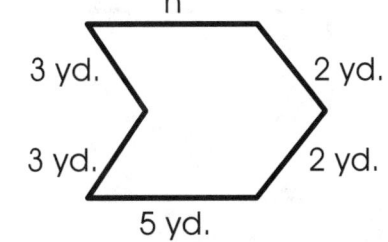

P = 21 yd., n = _____

4.

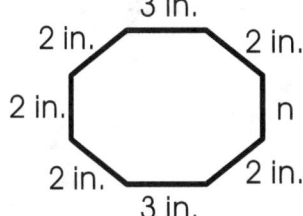

P = 18 in, n = _____

5.

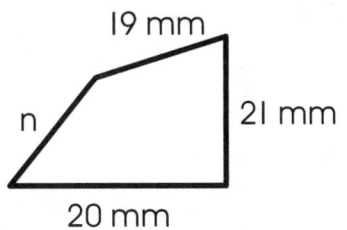

P = 78 mm, n = _____

6.

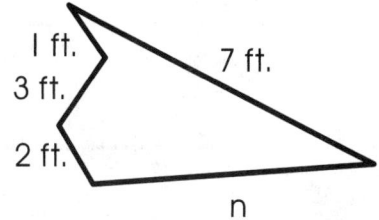

P = 19 ft., n = _____

7.

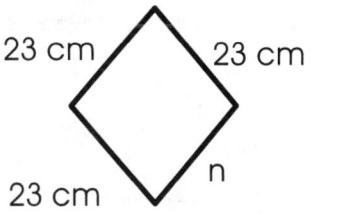

P = 92 cm, n = _____

8.

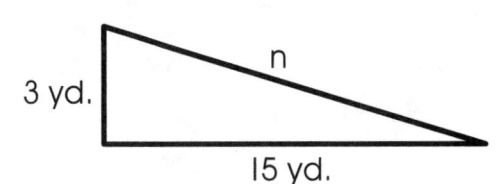

P = 36 yd., n = _____

9.

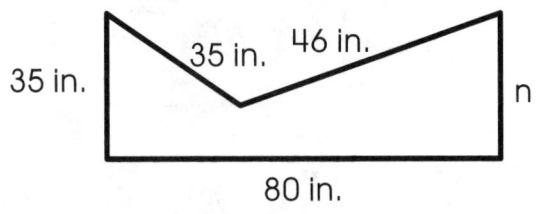

P = 231 in., n = _____

10.

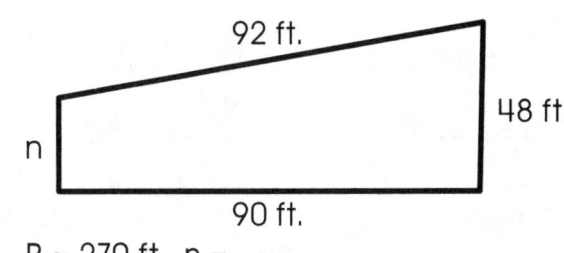

P = 270 ft., n = _____

Name: _____ Date: _____

Finding the Perimeter of Squares and Rectangles Using Multiplication

Area, Perimeter, and Volume

Example: P = (2 • l) + (2 • w)

P = (2 • 8 cm) + (2 • 4 cm)

P = 16 cm + 8 cm

P = 24 cm

l = 8 cm

w = 4 cm

Use the formula P = (2 • l) + (2 • w) and the steps shown in the example to find the perimeter of each quadrilateral with congruent opposite sides. (l = length, w = width)

1.

4 yd.

2 yd.

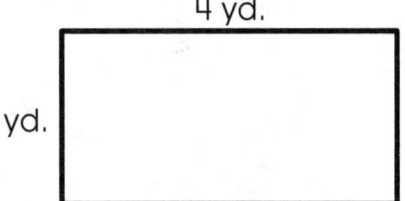

P = _____

2.

6 ft.

3 ft.

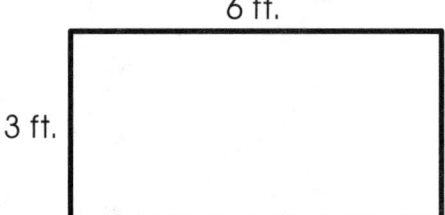

P = _____

3.

19 ft.

5 ft.

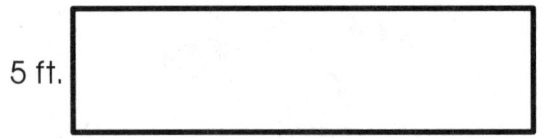

P = _____

4.

6 in.

7 in.

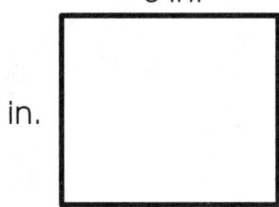

P = _____

5.

8 in.

8 in.

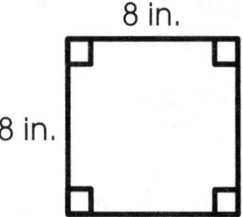

P = _____

6.

12 mm

9 mm

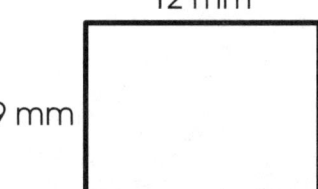

P = _____

7.

1 ft.

14 ft.

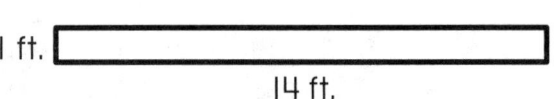

P = _____

8.

9 mm

3 mm

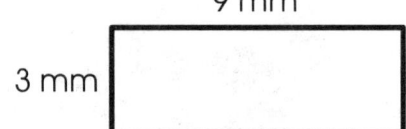

P = _____

Name: _____ Date: _____

Perimeter Word Problems

1. Mrs. Young's tennis court is a rectangle that is 30 feet wide by 70 feet long. What is the perimeter?

   _____

2. A rectangular pool table is 84 inches long and 36 inches wide. What is the perimeter?

   _____

3. A sports court is a rectangle. The sides are 260 feet long and 120 feet wide. What is the perimeter of the sports court?

   _____

4. A flower bed is rectangular. It is 8 feet long and 4 feet wide. How much fencing is needed to go around the flower bed?

   _____

5. A mirror is 26 inches wide and 30 inches long. How much framing is needed to encase the mirror?

   _____

6. A square tile has sides that are 15 inches each. What is the perimeter?

   _____

7. A hexagon has sides that are 5 millimeters. What is the perimeter?

   _____

8. An equilateral triangle has sides that are 21 feet. What is the perimeter?

   _____

9. A rectangular table measures 7 feet by 3 feet. What is the perimeter?

   _____

10. A square pool has sides that are 10 feet each. What is the perimeter?

   _____

Name: _____ Date: _____

Exploring Area   Area, Perimeter, and Volume

Area is the number of **square units** enclosed within a boundary. Area is measured in different units such as square feet or square centimeters. For example, there are 14 square units in this figure.

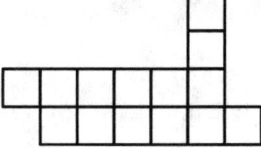

Find the area of each figure.

1.

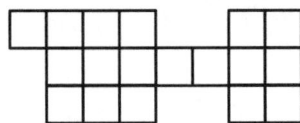

_____ square units

2.

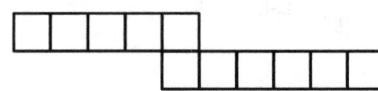

_____ square units

3.

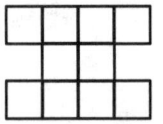

_____ square units

4.

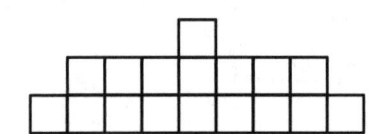

_____ square units

5.

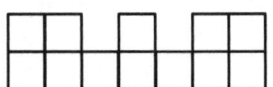

_____ square units

6.

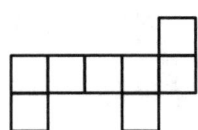

_____ square units

7.

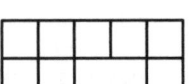

_____ square units

8.

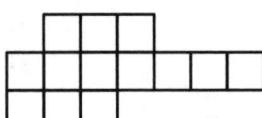

_____ square units

9.

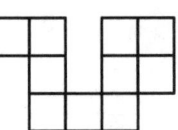

_____ square units

10.

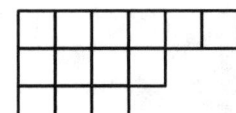

_____ square units

Name: _____ Date: _____

Counting Square Units

Area, Perimeter, and Volume

The area of a figure can be determined by counting its number of square units.

1	2	3
4	5	6
7	8	9

Count how many square units form each area.

1.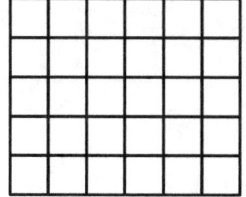

_____

2.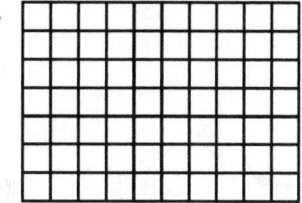

_____

3.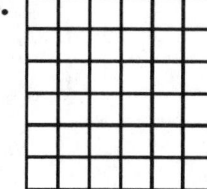

_____

4.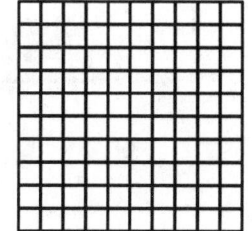

_____

5.

_____

6.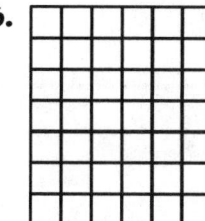

_____

7.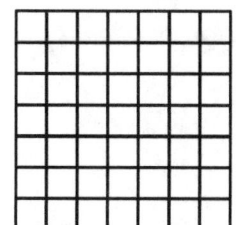

_____

8.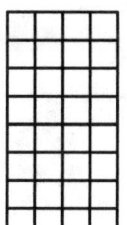

_____

9.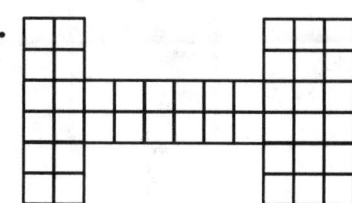

_____

10.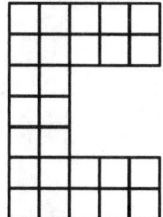

_____

11.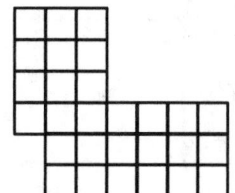

_____

12.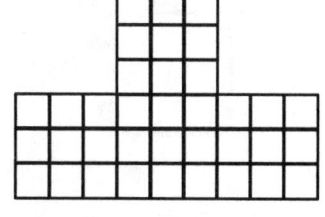

_____

Name: _____   Date: _____

Area of Squares and Rectangles   Area, Perimeter, and Volume

Calculating Area of a Square or Rectangle

The **area** of a figure tells how many square units are needed to cover the figure. Area can be measured in different units, such as square feet, square meters, or square inches.

Square $A = s^2$ (or $s \cdot s$)   **Rectangle** $A = lw$

Find the area of each figure in units squared (yd.^{2}, ft.^{2}, mm^2, etc.).

1.
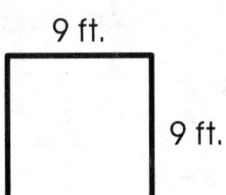
9 ft.
9 ft.

A = _____

2.
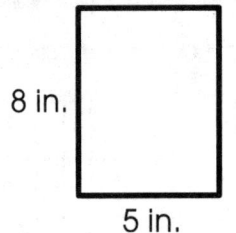
8 in.
5 in.

A = _____

3.
6 mm
2 mm

A = _____

4.
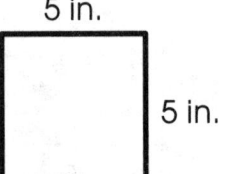
21 cm
8 cm

A = _____

5.
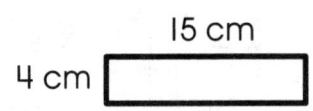
6 yd.
6 yd.

A = _____

6.
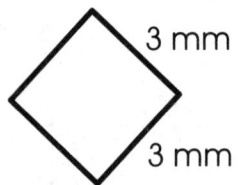
19 ft.
4 ft.

A = _____

7.
5 in.
5 in.

A = _____

8.
15 cm
4 cm

A = _____

9.
3 mm
3 mm

A = _____

10.
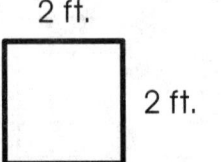
2 ft.
2 ft.

A = _____

11.
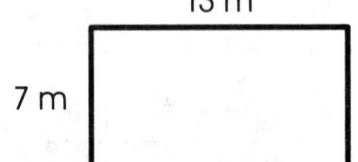
13 m
7 m

A = _____

12.
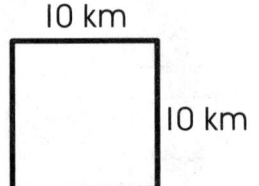
10 km
10 km

A = _____

Name: _____ Date: _____

Perimeter and Area of Rectangles Table

Area, Perimeter, and Volume

Complete the table. Then, answer the questions below.

Rectangle	Width (inches)	Perimeter (inches)	Length (inches)	Area (inches)
A	1	6		2
B	2		4	8
C	3	18	6	
D	4	24		32
E	5	30	10	
F	6		12	72
G	7	42		98

1. Which rectangle in the table has the greatest area? Does it also have the greatest perimeter?

   _____

   _____

2. Describe the pattern in the lengths and widths.

   _____

   _____

3. If you double the length and width of a rectangle, what happens to the area?

   _____

   _____

4. If you double the length and width of a rectangle, what happens to the perimeter?

   _____

   _____

5. Are the area and perimeter directly related to each other? Explain.

   _____

   _____

Changing the Area and Perimeter   Area, Perimeter, and Volume

Change each figure on the left to make another figure that has the same area but a larger perimeter. Draw the new figure on the dot grid to the right.

1.   A = 6 units^2 A = _____

P = 12 units   P = _____

2.   A = 6 units^2 A = _____

P = 12 units   P = _____

Now, change each figure below to make another figure that has the same area but a smaller perimeter. Draw the new figure on the dot gride to the right.

3.   A = 6 units^2 A = _____

P = 14 units   P = _____

4.   A = 6 units^2 A = _____

P = 14 units   P = _____

Draw three more figures that have different perimeters but the same area on the dot grids below.

A = _____   P = _____   P = _____   P = _____

5.   **6.**   **7.**

Area of Parallelograms
Calculating Area of a Parallelogram
Area = bh, where b = base and
h = height. (Height must form a right angle
with a base.)

Area, Perimeter, and Volume

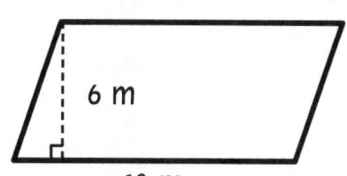

A = bh
A = 10 m • 6 m
A = 60 m²

Find the area of each parallelogram in units squared (yd.², ft.², mm², etc.).

1.

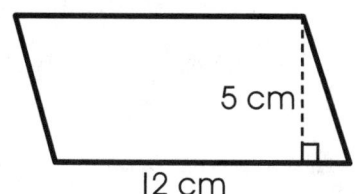

A = _____

2.

A = _____

3.

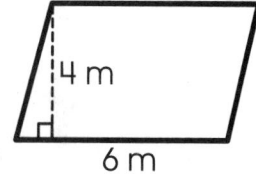

A = _____

4.

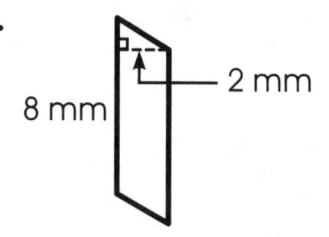

A = _____

5.

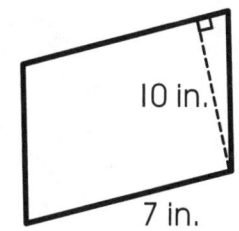

A = _____

6.

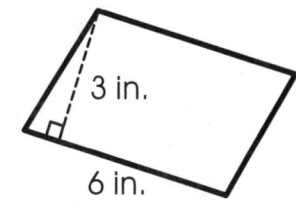

A = _____

7.

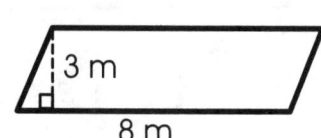

A = _____

8.

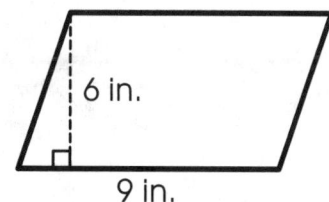

A = _____

9.

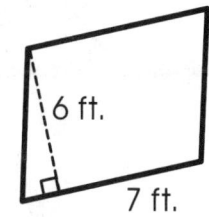

A = _____

10.

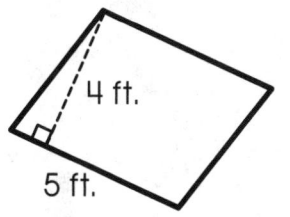

A = _____

11.

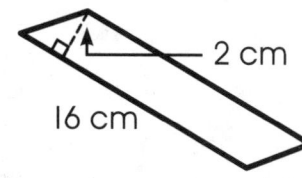

A = _____

12.

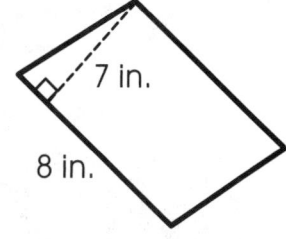

A = _____

Name: _____ Date: _____

Area of Triangles

Calculating Area of a Triangle

Area = ½(bh), where b = base and
h = height. (Height must form a
right angle with a base.)

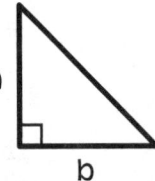

Area, Perimeter, and Volume

$A = \frac{1}{2}(bh)$

$A = \frac{1}{2}(6\text{ m} \cdot 10\text{ m})$

$A = \frac{1}{2}(60\text{ m}^2)$

$A = 30\text{ m}^2$

Find the area of each triangle in units squared (yd.², ft.², mm², etc.).

1.

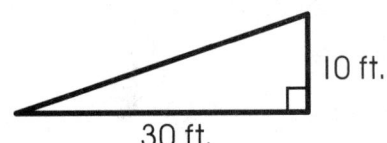

30 ft. 10 ft.

A = _____

2.

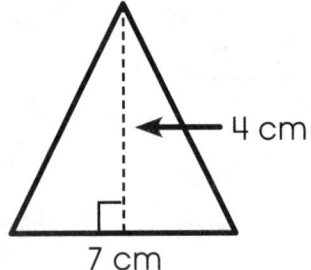

4 cm

7 cm

A = _____

3.

18 km 15 km

A = _____

4.

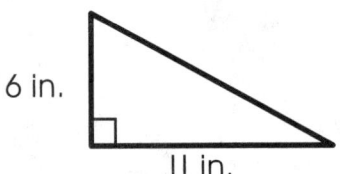

6 in.

11 in.

A = _____

5.

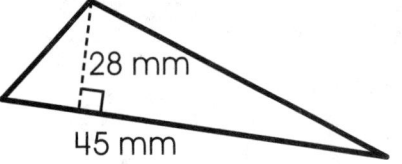

28 mm

45 mm

A = _____

6.

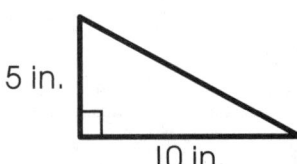

5 in.

10 in.

A = _____

7.

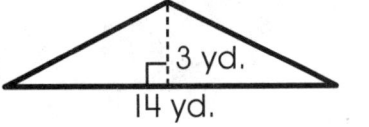

3 yd.

14 yd.

A = _____

8.

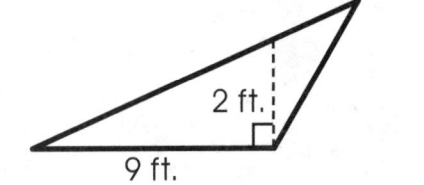

2 ft.

9 ft.

A = _____

Area of Triangles Table

Area, Perimeter, and Volume

Complete the table to show the base, height, and area of each triangle. Use the space to the right to work the problems.

	Base	Height	Area
1.	6 cm	2 cm	
2.	8 cm	6 cm	
3.	7 cm	2 cm	
4.	8 cm		56 cm²
5.	9 cm	4 cm	
6.	10 cm		70 cm²
7.	7 cm	6 cm	
8.		3 cm	18 cm²
9.		9 cm	54 cm²
10.	10 cm	8 cm	
11.	12 cm		72 cm²
12.		3 cm	27 cm²
13.	11 cm	4 cm	
14.		9 cm	108 cm²
15.		4 cm	28 cm²
16.	10 cm	9 cm	
17.	11 cm	6 cm	
18.	9 cm		72 cm²
19.	6 cm		30 cm²
20.		9 cm	99 cm²
21.	8 cm		40 cm²
22.	12 cm	8 cm	
23.	9 cm	6 cm	
24.	5 cm		35 cm²
25.		8 cm	88 cm²

Name: _____ Date: _____

Area of Trapezoids

Calculating Area of a Trapezoid

Area = $\frac{1}{2}h(b_1 + b_2)$, where b = base and h = height. (Height must form a right angle with a base.)

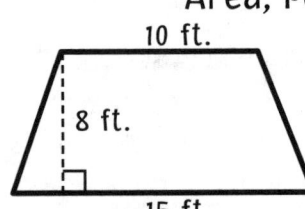

$A = \frac{1}{2}h(b_1 + b_2)$
$A = \frac{1}{2}8\text{ ft.}(10\text{ ft.} + 15\text{ ft.})$
$A = \frac{1}{2}8\text{ ft.}(25\text{ ft.})$
$A = 4\text{ ft.}(25\text{ ft.})$
$A = 100\text{ ft.}^2$

Find the area of each trapezoid in units squared (yd.², ft.², mm², etc.).

1.

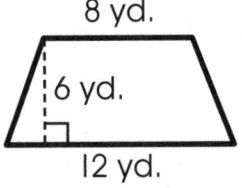

A = _____

2.

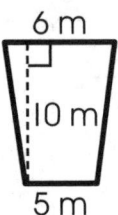

A = _____

3.

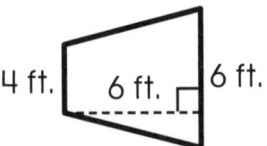

A = _____

4.

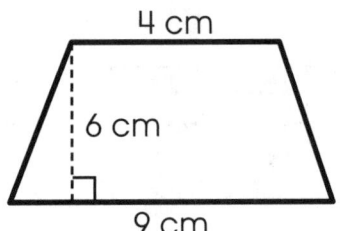

A = _____

5.

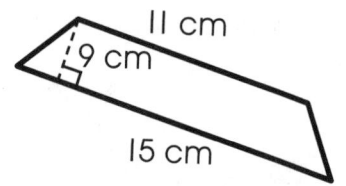

A = _____

6.

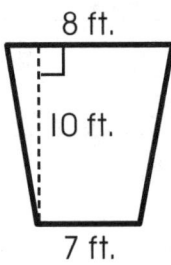

A = _____

7.

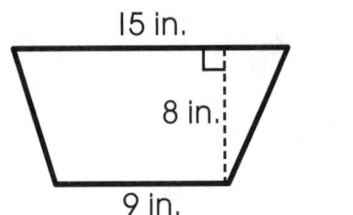

A = _____

8.

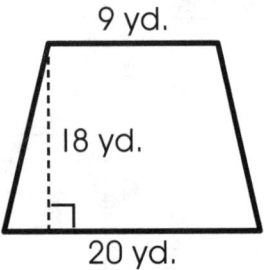

A = _____

Missing Area

Area, Perimeter, and Volume

Find the area of the shaded portion of each figure below in units squared (yd.², ft.², mm², etc.). Remember to subtract the known area from the total area.

1.

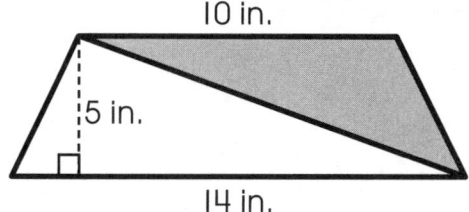

A = _____

2.

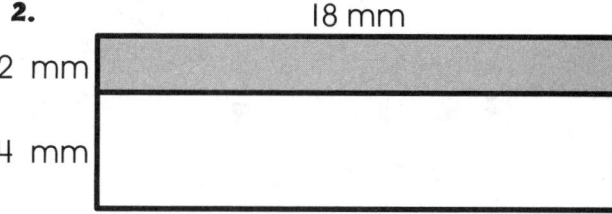

A = _____

3.

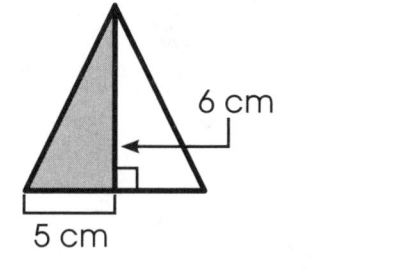

A = _____

4.

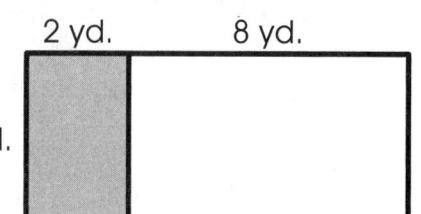

A = _____

5.

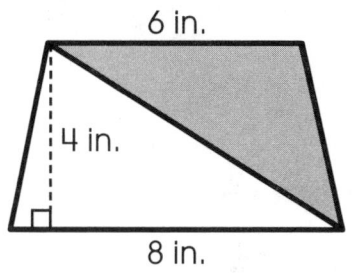

A = _____

6.

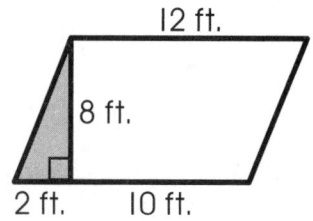

A = _____

7.

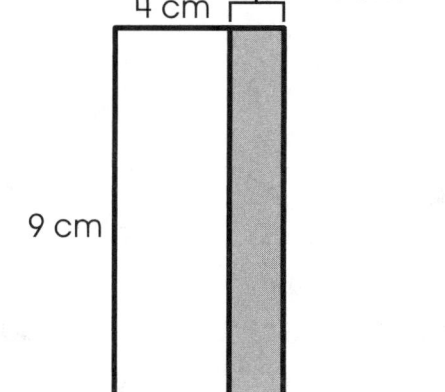

A = _____

8.

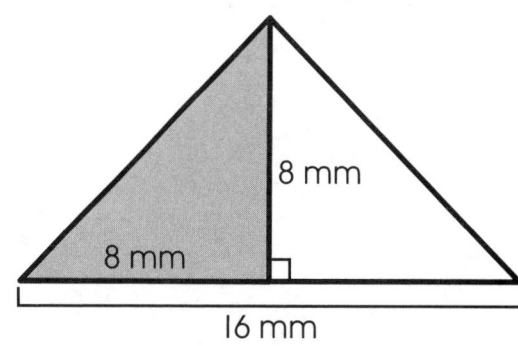

A = _____

Name: _____ Date: _____

Area Word Problems
Area, Perimeter, and Volume

Using the formulas you have learned, solve the word problems below.

1. A parallelogram-shaped garden has an area of 42 square yards and a height of 6 yards. Find the base.

   _____

2. The area of a parallelogram is 64 square inches, and the height is 16 inches. Find the base.

   _____

3. Find the area of a parallelogram with a base of 4 meters and a height of 9 meters.

   _____

4. Find the area of a trapezoid with bases of 5 feet and 7 feet, and a height of 3 feet.

   _____

5. Find the area of a trapezoid with bases of 12 meters and 6 meters, and a height of 5 meters.

   _____

6. The area of a trapezoid is 48 square inches, and the bases are 4 inches and 8 inches. Find the height.

   _____

Name: _____ Date: _____

Area and Perimeter Word Problems   Area, Perimeter, and Volume

Using the formulas you have learned, solve the word problems below.

1. A playing card has a length of 10 centimeters and a width of 5 centimeters. What is its perimeter?

   _____

2. A triangular-shaped yard has a base of 25 meters and a height of 12 meters. What is its area?

   _____

3. If one side of a stop sign measures 12 inches, then what is its perimeter?

   _____

4. A trapezoid has bases of 9 centimeters and 6 centimeters, and a height of 4 centimeters. What is its area?

   _____

5. A rectangular piece of paper has a width of 16 inches and an area of 192 square inches. What is its length?

   _____

6. A square garden has a side of 22 meters. How many meters of fence are needed to enclose the garden?

   _____

Exploring Volume

Area, Perimeter, and Volume

Volume tells the number of cubic units inside a figure. Each box represents one cubic unit.

4 cubic units

Write the number of cubic units in each figure.

1.

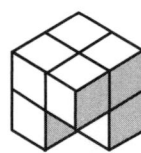

cubic units: _____

2.

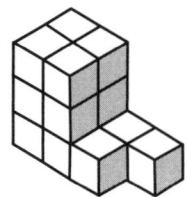

cubic units: _____

3.

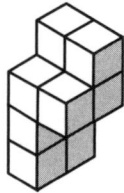

cubic units: _____

4.

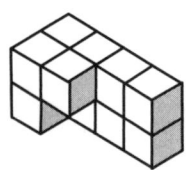

cubic units: _____

5.

cubic units: _____

6.

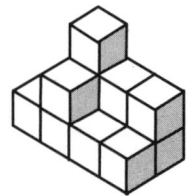

cubic units: _____

Use the figure to the right to answer the questions below.

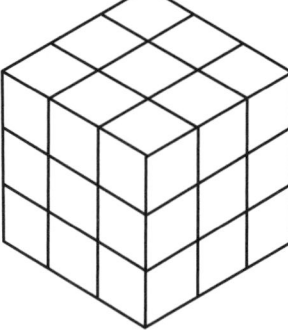

7. If you painted the front, top, and bottom of the figure, how many cubic units would have one side painted?

_____

8. How many cubic units would have two sides painted?

_____

9. How many cubic units would have no paint on them?

_____

Volume of Rectangular Prisms
Area, Perimeter, and Volume

Calculating Volume of a Rectangular Prism

Volume = lwh, where l = length,
w = width, and h = height.

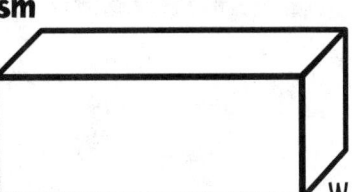

h = 2 ft.

l = 8 ft.

w = 2 ft.

$V = lwh$
$V = 8 \text{ ft.} \cdot 2 \text{ft.} \cdot 2 \text{ ft.}$
$V = 32 \text{ ft.}^3$

Use the formula to find the volume of each figure in units cubed (yd.³, ft.³, mm³, etc.).

1.

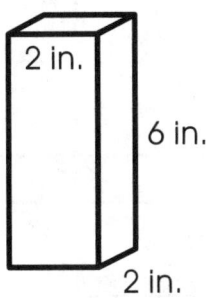

2 in.
6 in.
2 in.

V = _____

2.

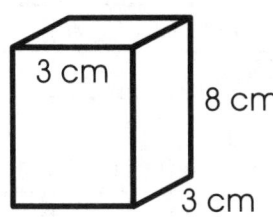

3 cm
8 cm
3 cm

V = _____

3.

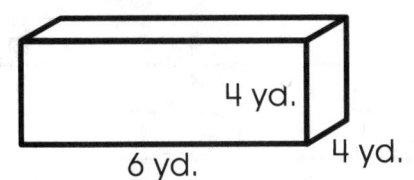

4 yd.
6 yd.
4 yd.

V = _____

4.

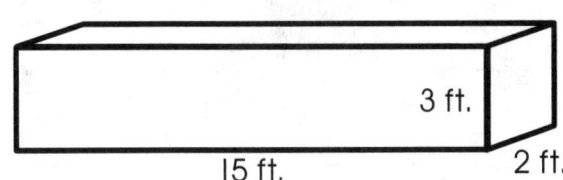

3 ft.
15 ft.
2 ft.

V = _____

5.

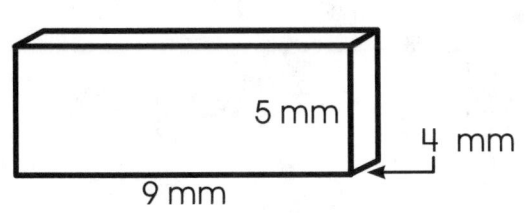

5 mm
4 mm
9 mm

V = _____

6.

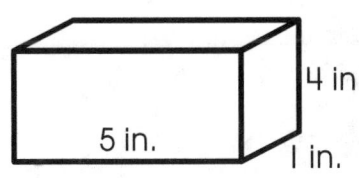

4 in.
5 in.
1 in.

V = _____

7.

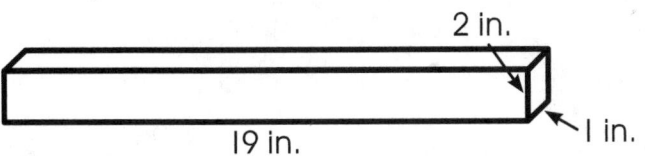

2 in.
19 in.
1 in.

V = _____

8.

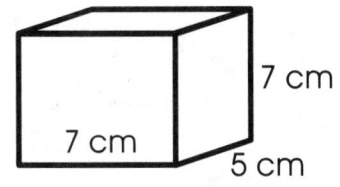

7 cm
7 cm
5 cm

V = _____

Name: _____ Date: _____

Volume of Rectangular Prisms Table   Area, Perimeter, and Volume

Complete the table to show length, width, height, and volume of each rectangular prism. Use the space below to work the problems. Remember the formula for finding volume is V = lwh.

	Length	Width	Height	Volume
1.		4 mm	6 mm	48 mm³
2.	8 mm	5 mm	1 mm	
3.	2 mm	9 mm	4 mm	
4.		3 mm	18 mm	162 mm³
5.	12 mm	2 mm		72 mm³
6.		3 mm	3 mm	279 mm³
7.	2 mm	11 mm	4 mm	
8.	6 mm	9 mm		108 mm³
9.	5 mm	4 mm	8 mm	
10.	15 mm		3 mm	270 mm³
11.	12 mm	3 mm	3 mm	
12.	23 mm	3 mm		69 mm³
13.		5 mm	11 mm	550 mm³
14.	9 mm		20 mm	540 mm³
15.	2 mm	14 mm	6 mm	
16.		1 mm	15 mm	60 mm³

Name: _____   Date: _____

Volume Multiple Choice   Area, Perimeter, and Volume

Circle the correct answer for each problem.

1. What is the volume of a cereal box if the dimensions are a length of 2 in., a height of 14 in., and a width of 2 in.?

A. 18 cubic in.   B. 24 cubic in.   C. 56 cubic in.   D. 48 cubic in.

2. A baby's block measures 12 cm. What is the volume?

A. 1,728 cubic cm   B. 1,200 cubic cm   C. 144 cubic cm   D. 36 cubic cm

3. A juice box measures measures 4 cm in length, 10 cm in height, and 5 cm in width. What is the volume?

A. 300 cubic cm   B. 190 cubic cm   C. 19 cubic cm   D. 200 cubic cm

4. The dimensions of a toy box are 2 ft. high, 2 ft. wide, and 3 ft. long. What is the volume of the toy box?

A. 12 cubic ft.   B. 7 cubic ft.   C. 15 cubic ft.   D. 22 cubic ft.

5. The new sandbox measures 12 ft. x 1 ft. x 6 ft. How much room is there for sand?

A. 19 cubic ft.   B. 72 cubic ft.   C. 52 cubic ft.   D. 22 cubic ft.

6. The shed in the James's yard is 16 yd. long, 4 yd. wide, and 5 yd. high. What is the space inside the shed?

A. 32 cubic yd.   B. 25 cubic yd.   C. 225 cubic yd.   D. 320 cubic yd.

Circumference and Pi (π)   Area, Perimeter, and Volume

Calculating Circumference $C = \pi d$ or $C = 2\pi r$

The **circumference** is the distance around a circle. To find the circumference of a circle, multiply π (which always equals approximately 3.14) times the diameter or multiply two times π (3.14) times the radius (r).

Follow the steps to complete the table below.

1. Measure the circumference, or the distance around each circle by carefully wrapping a piece of string around it. Then, straighten the string and measure it with a centimeter ruler. Write each measurement on the table.

2. Measure the diameter of each circle and write it on the table.

3. Divide each circle's circumference by the diameter and write the answer in the last column. What pattern do you see?

Circle	Circumference (C)	Diameter (d)	C ÷ d
A			
B			
C			
D			
E			

A.

B.

C.

E.

D.

Circumference of a Circle   Area, Perimeter, and Volume

The **circumference** of a circle is the length of the boundary of the circle. The circumference can be computed by multiplying the diameter by pi (π), a number that is a little more than 3.14.

C = circumference, π = 3.14 or 22/7, d = diameter, and r = radius.

C = πd   or   C = 2πr

C = 3.14(8 mm)   C = 2(3.14)(4 mm)

C = 25.12 mm   C = 6.28(4 mm)

                                   C = 25.12 mm

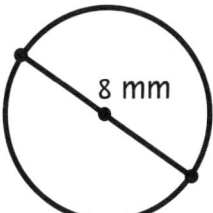

Find the circumference of each circle.

1.  16 in.

C = _____

2.  18 km

C = _____

3. 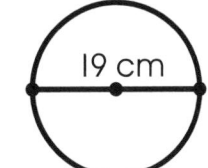 19 cm

C = _____

4. 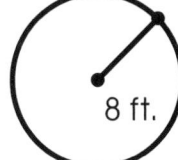 8 ft.

C = _____

5.  22 cm

C = _____

6.  5 m

C = _____

7. 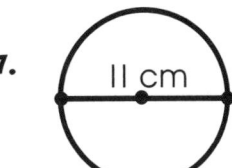 11 cm

C = _____

8.  14 in.

C = _____

Solving for the Circumference of a Circle

Area, Perimeter, and Volume

Use the information about each circle to solve for the circumference. Remember these formulas: Diameter = 2r   Circumference = πd or 2πr

1.   11 cm

_____

2.   4 mm

_____

3.   18 ft.

_____

4.   16 mm

_____

5.   8 in.

_____

6.   20 cm

_____

7.   22 yd.

_____

8.   9 in.

_____

9.   31 yd.

_____

10.   3 in.

_____

11.   6 ft.

_____

12.   12 ft.

_____

13.   Radius is 17 cm.

_____

14.   Radius is 6 ft.

_____

15.   Diameter is 9 in.

_____

16.   Diameter is 4 yd.

_____

17.   Radius is 16 mm.

_____

18.   Diameter is 12 cm.

_____

19.   Diameter is 35 ft.

_____

20.   Radius is 95 in.

_____

21.   Diameter is 8 yd.

_____

Name: _____   Date: _____

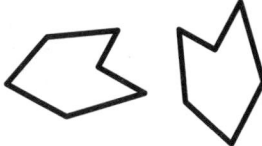

Circle the correct congruent figure for the first figure in each row.

1.	⬠ flag	⚐	M	⬠ flag	M
2.	△	△	△	△	△
3.	trapezoid	△	trapezoid	trapezoid	trapezoid
4.	pentagon	pentagon	pentagon	pentagon	pentagon
5.	✚	✖	✚	✚	✚
6.	hexagon	hexagon	hexagon	hexagon	hexagon
7.	▱	▭	▱	△	▱
8.	✕	✚	⋈	∨	✕

Similar Figures
Congruence, Symmetry, and Transformations

Similar figures are the same shape but not necessarily the same size.

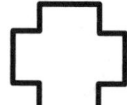

These figures are similar.

These figures are not similar.

Circle the similar figure for the first figure in each row.

Name: _____   Date: _____

Congruent vs. Similar Figures

Congruence, Symmetry, and Transformations

Similar figures are the same shape but not necessarily the same size. Congruent figures are the same shape and also the same size.

Look at each pair of figures and write *congruent* or *similar*

1.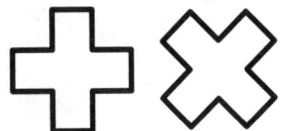

_____

2.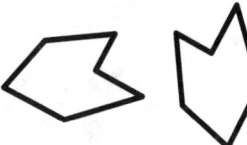

_____

3.

_____

4.

_____

5.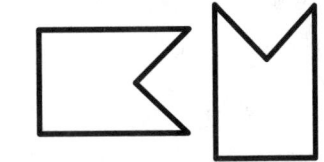

_____

6.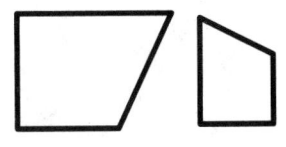

_____

7.

_____

8.

_____

9.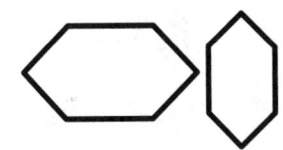

_____

10.

_____

11.

_____

12.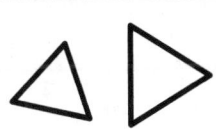

_____

13.

_____

14.

_____

15.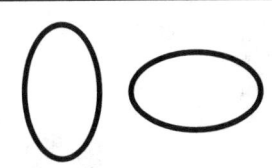

_____

Name: _____ Date: _____

Butterfly Symmetry — Congruence, Symmetry, and Transformations

Butterflies are interesting insects. One of the most interesting things about them is that the left side of a butterfly's body is a mirror image of the right side. This means that the right and left sides of a butterfly's body are **symmetrical**. The line that divides the butterfly into two mirror-image parts is the **line of symmetry**.

Draw the line of symmetry on each butterfly.

1.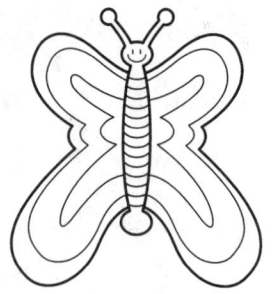

2.

3.

4.

5.

6.

7. Draw a butterfly below and color it. Remember to make both sides of the butterfly's body mirror images so that they are symmetrical.

Line Symmetry

Congruence, Symmetry, and Transformations

A figure has **line symmetry** if it can be folded along a line so that the two halves are mirror images.

These figures have line symmetry. The heart has one line of symmetry. The rectangle has two lines of symmetry.

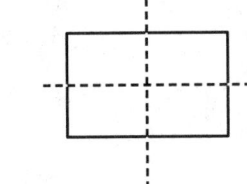

These figures do not have line symmetry.

Determine if the following figures have line symmetry and write *yes* or *no*. If *yes*, draw all of the lines of symmetry.

1.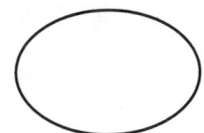
_____

2.
_____

3.
_____

4.
_____

5.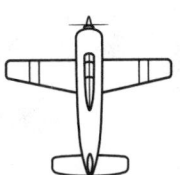
_____

6.
_____

7.
_____

8.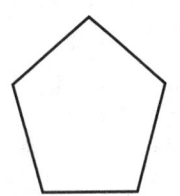
_____

9.
_____

10. Draw a figure that has at least one line of symmetry that is not shown on this page. Then, draw the line or lines of symmetry.

Snowflake Symmetry   Congruence, Symmetry, and Transformations

Below are basic snowflakes. They are made up of eight rays with one common endpoint. Create a pattern on one ray and then draw it on the rest of the rays to make a symmetrical snowflake. The first one is started for you.

1.

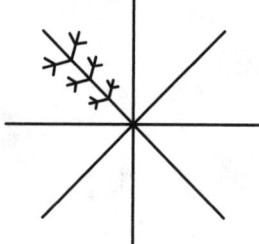

2.

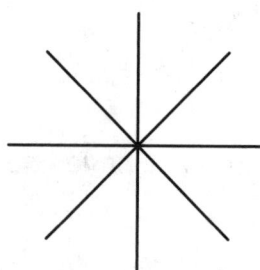

3.

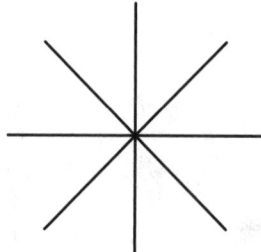

4.

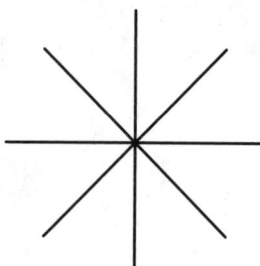

5.

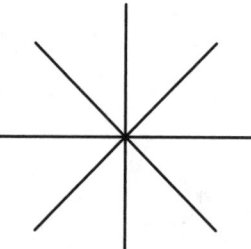

6.

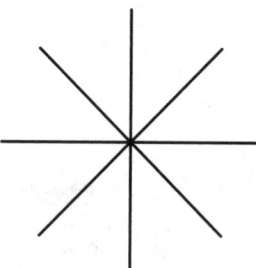

7.

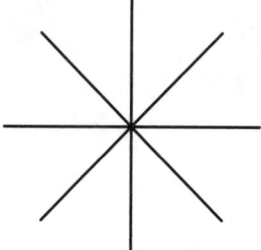

8.

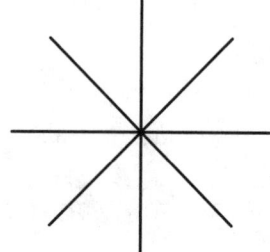

Drawing Figures with Symmetry

Congruence, Symmetry, and Transformations

Complete each design to show symmetry. Remember, both sides of each line of symmetry need to be congruent.

1.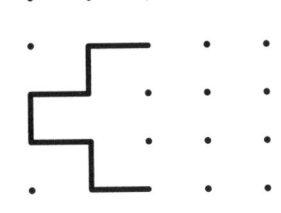

2.

3.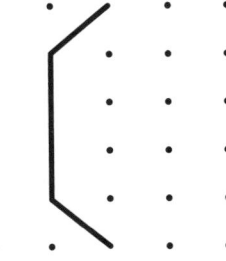

4.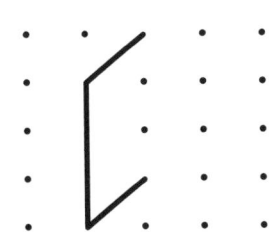

5.

6.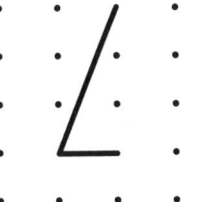

7.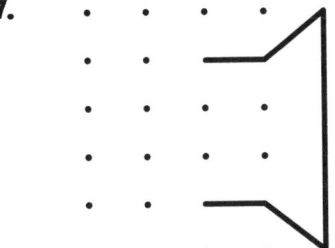

8.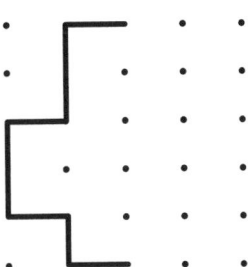

9.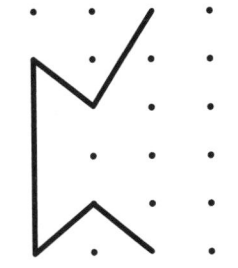

10.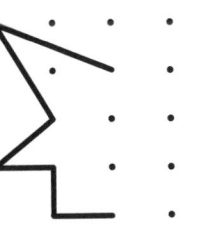

11.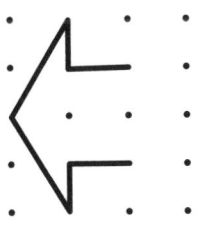

12.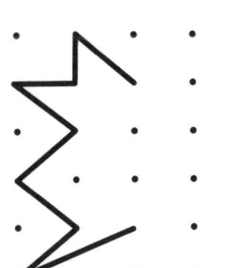

13.

14.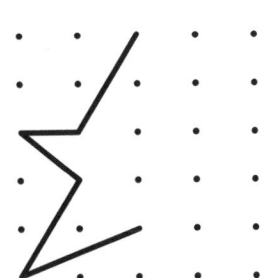

15.

More Drawing Figures with Symmetry

Congruence, Symmetry, and Transformations

Draw your own figures with correct lines of symmetry. The first one is done for you.

1. Draw your figure.

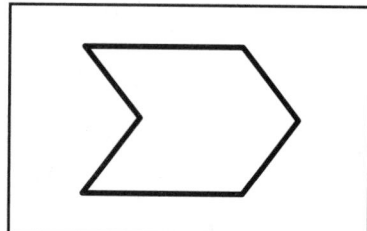

Draw the correct line of symmetry.

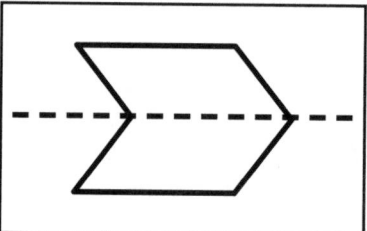

2.

3.

4.

5.

Drawing Lines of Symmetry

Congruence, Symmetry, and Transformations

A **line of symmetry** is any line that can be drawn through a figure that divides it into two mirror images.

Draw lines of symmetry on the figures below. Some figures will have one line of symmetry, some will have multiple lines of symmetry, and some may have none.

1.

2.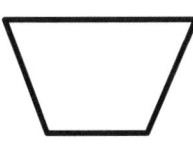

3.

4.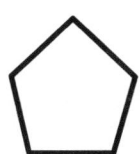

5.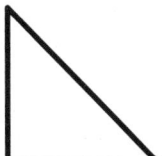

6.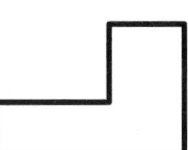

7.

8.

9.

10.

11.

12.

More Drawing Lines of Symmetry

Congruence, Symmetry, and Transformations

Some objects have more than one line of symmetry. A regular hexagon has six lines of symmetry.

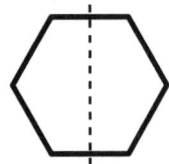 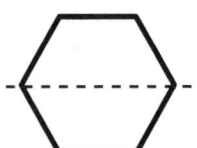   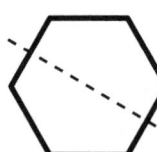 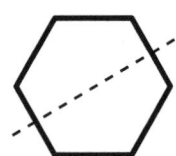

Decide whether these figures have one line of symmetry, two lines of symmetry, or no lines of symmetry. Write *one*, *two*, or *none*. Then, draw the line or lines.

1.

2.

3.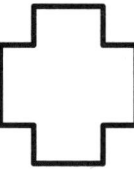

_____   _____   _____

4.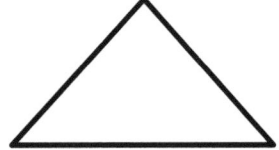

5.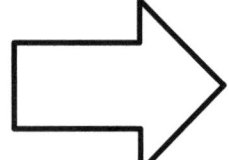

6.

_____   _____   _____

7.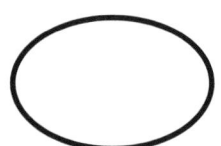

8.

9.

_____   _____   _____

10.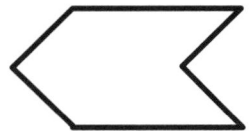

11.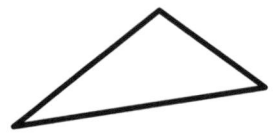

12.

_____   _____   _____

Lines of Symmetry: Mixed Practice
Congruence, Symmetry, and Transformations

Draw the line or lines of symmetry on each object. Then, write the number of lines of symmetry that each object has.

1.

Number of lines _____

2.

Number of lines _____

3.

Number of lines _____

4.

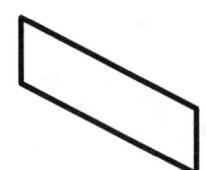

Number of lines _____

5.

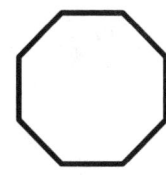

Number of lines _____

6.

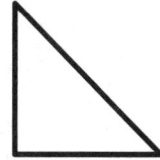

Number of lines _____

7.

Number of lines _____

8.

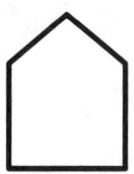

Number of lines _____

9.

Number of lines _____

10.

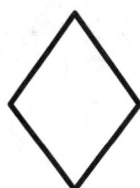

Number of lines _____

11.

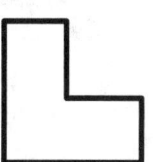

Number of lines _____

12.

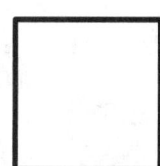

Number of lines _____

13.

Number of lines _____

14.

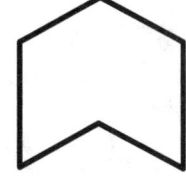

Number of lines _____

15.

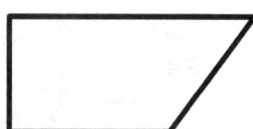

Number of lines _____

Slides, Turns, and Flips

Congruence, Symmetry, and Transformations

A **slide** moves a figure to a new position. Every point on the figure moves the same distance in the same direction.

A **turn** rotates a figure around a position without changing its size or shape.

A **flip** flips a figure over a line, making a mirror image of the original figure.

These are examples of **transformation**—moving a geometric figure from one position to another, according to a rule.

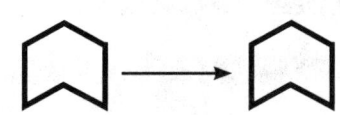

Determine how each figure was moved. Write *slide*, *turn*, or *flip*.

1.

_____

2.

_____

3.

_____

4.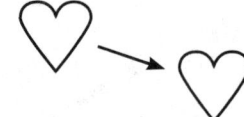

_____

5.

_____

6.

_____

7.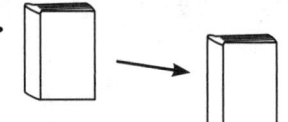

_____

8.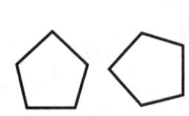

_____

9.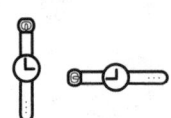

_____

10.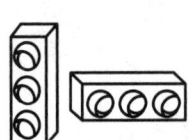

_____

11.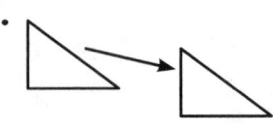

_____

12.

_____

13.

_____

14.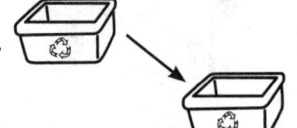

_____

15.

_____

16.

_____

Identifying Slides, Flips, and Turns

Congruence, Symmetry, and Transformations

Circle the correct transformation for each set of figures below. If none of these transformations have been performed, then circle *none*.

1. 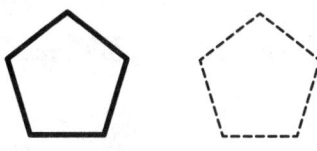 slide flip turn none

2.  slide flip turn none

3. 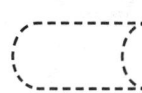 slide flip turn none

4. 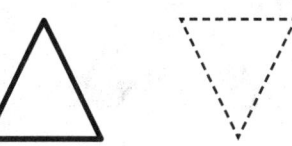 slide flip turn none

5. 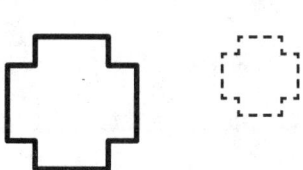 slide flip turn none

6.  slide flip turn none

7. 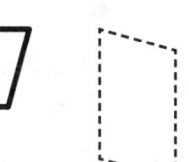 slide flip turn none

8. 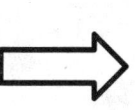 slide flip turn none

Drawing Slides, Flips, and Turns

Congruence, Symmetry, and Transformations

Turns can be described in terms of degrees.

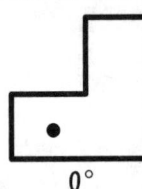 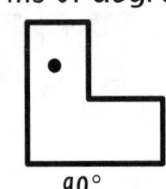  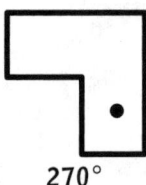

| 0° | 90° | 180° | 270° |

Draw each figure according to the directions.

1. Draw a 90° turn.

2. Draw a flip.

3. Draw a 90° turn.

4. Draw a 270° turn.

5. Draw a slide.

6. Draw a 270° turn.

7. Draw a 90° turn.

8. Draw a 180° turn.

9. Draw a slide.

10. Draw a flip.

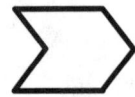

11. Draw a 180° turn.

12. Draw a 270° turn.

Turns by Degrees
Congruence, Symmetry, and Transformations

Look at each figure in its original position and identify the transformation. Write *flip*, *slide*, *90° turn*, *180° turn*, or *270° turn*.

1.

_____

2.

_____

3.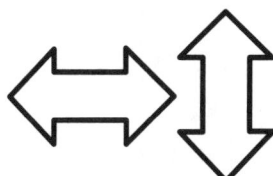

_____

4.

_____

5.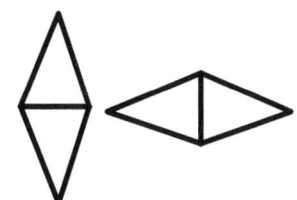

_____

6.

_____

Draw each figure according to the directions.

7. Draw a 90°, clockwise turn.

8. Draw a flip.

9. Draw a 270°, counterclockwise turn.

10. Draw a flip and slide.

11. Draw a 180°, clockwise turn.

12. Draw a slide.

Name: _____ Date: _____

1. Do the figures appear to be similar? If so, are they also congruent?

_____

2. Explain how to tell if a figure has symmetry. _____

_____

3. When are two similar figures also congruent? _____

_____

4. Can an obtuse triangle and a right triangle ever be similar? _____

Explain. _____

_____

5. Can an obtuse triangle and a right triangle ever be congruent? _____

Explain. _____

_____

6. If two triangles are similar and one is an obtuse scalene triangle, is the other one also an obtuse scalene triangle? _____

Explain. _____

_____

7. If this figure is flipped over a dotted line and then turned 180°, which figure below shows the result?

   A.    B.    C.    D.

8. Which drawing shows this figure turned 180°?

   A.    B.    C.    D.

Name: _____ Date: _____

1. Circle the triangles that appear to be similar.

A.    B.    C.    D.

2. Circle the shapes that appear to be congruent.

A. 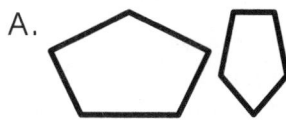   B.    C.    D.

3. Identify each figure's transformation. Write *turn*, *slide*, or *flip*.

A. 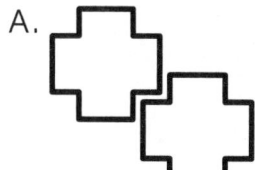   B.    C.

_____   _____   _____

4. Determine how many lines of symmetry the letters have. Then, draw the lines.

A.    B.    C.

5. Complete each drawing to create a symmetrical figure.

A. 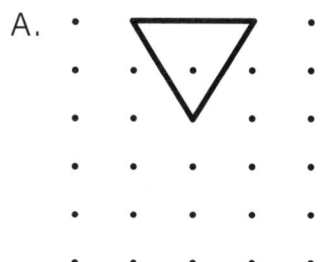   B. 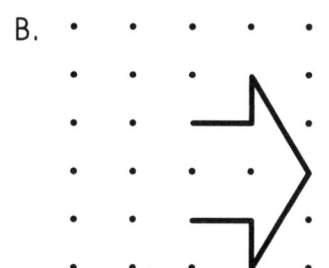   C.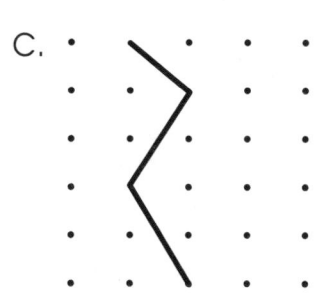

Name: _____ Date: _____

Tessellations

Congruence, Symmetry, and Transformations

A **tessellation** is an arrangement of plane figures (possibly a combination of figures like hexagons and triangles) to cover a surface without overlapping or leaving any gaps.

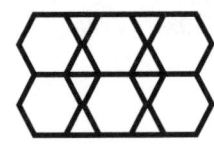

A **regular tessellation** is made of regular polygons that are all the same. In a regular tessellation, each vertex (the point where the corners meet) must look the same.

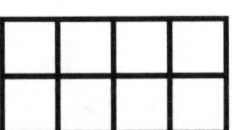

Determine if the following sets of figures are regular tessellations and write *yes* or *no*.

1.  _____

2.  _____

3. 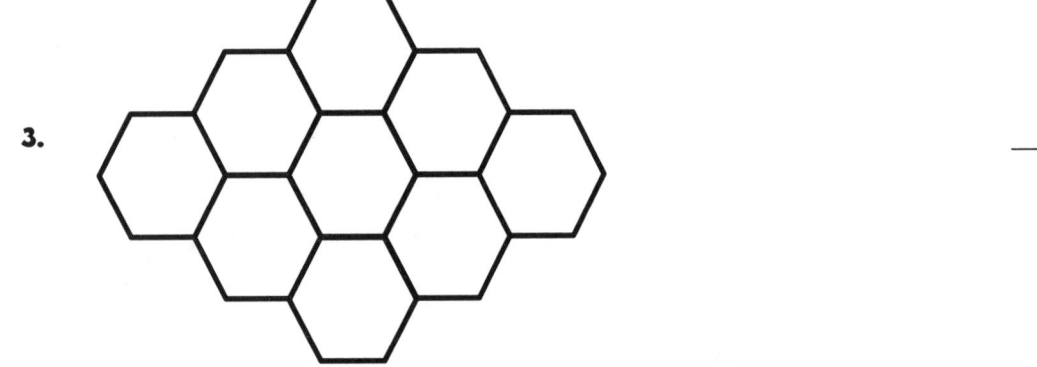 _____

Draw two tessellations using the given regular polygons. Be creative. Use flips, turns, and/or slides.

4.

5.

Name: _____ Date: _____

Designing Tessellations   Congruence, Symmetry, and Transformations

1. Use the space below to create a tessellation using a right triangle.

[ ]

2. Describe how the right triangle was moved to create the pattern.

_____

_____

3. Design a tessellation in the space below using two different figures. Try to fill the box with the chosen figures.

[ ]

4. What figures did you use? _____

5. How many sides does each figure have? _____

6. How were the figures moved to form a tessellation?_____

_____

7. Could the figures have been moved more than one way? Explain your answer.

_____

_____

_____

8. Define tessellation._____

_____

_____

Coordinate Graphing

To use a **coordinate grid**, always read the x-axis first. Read the y-axis second.

The **x-axis** runs from left to right.

The **y-axis** runs from bottom to top.

To describe the location of a point, use an **ordered pair** (x, y).

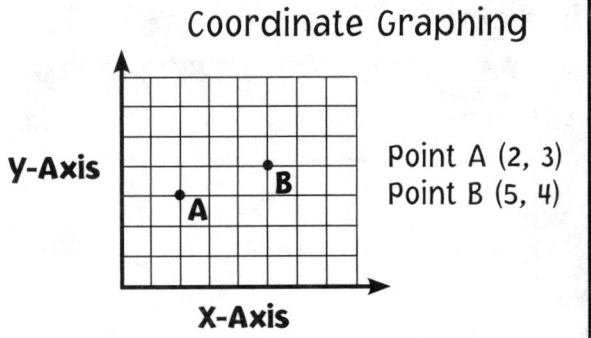

Coordinate Graphing

Point A (2, 3)
Point B (5, 4)

Plot the following ordered pairs by drawing and labeling each point on the coordinate grid.

1. A (0, 5)

2. B (1, 3)

3. C (2, 4)

4. D (7, 5)

5. E (8, 1)

6. F (7, 3)

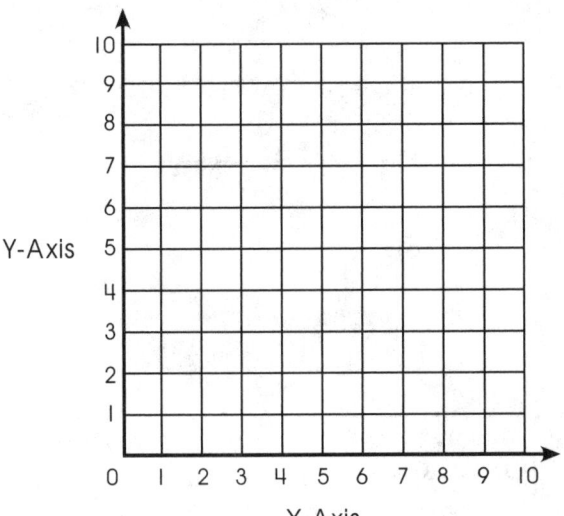

Identify the ordered pair for each point. Write the numbers for x and y.

7. A (____ , ____)

8. B (____ , ____)

9. C (____ , ____)

10. D (____ , ____)

11. E (____ , ____)

12. F (____ , ____)

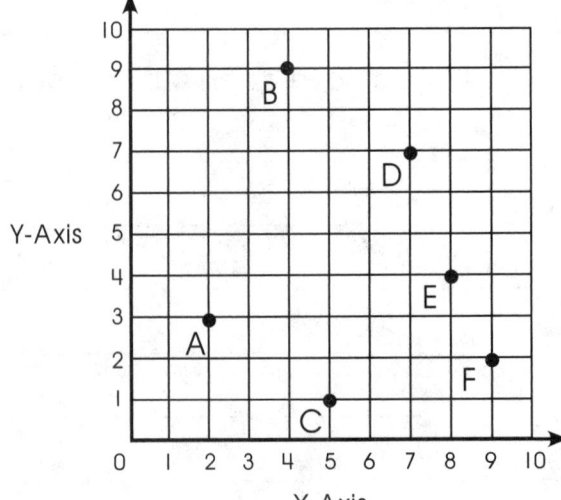

Coordinate Polygons

Coordinate Graphing

Plot the following ordered pairs on the coordinate grid. Then, connect the points to form a polygon.

1. (5, 8)

(5, 2)

(3, 5)

(7, 5)

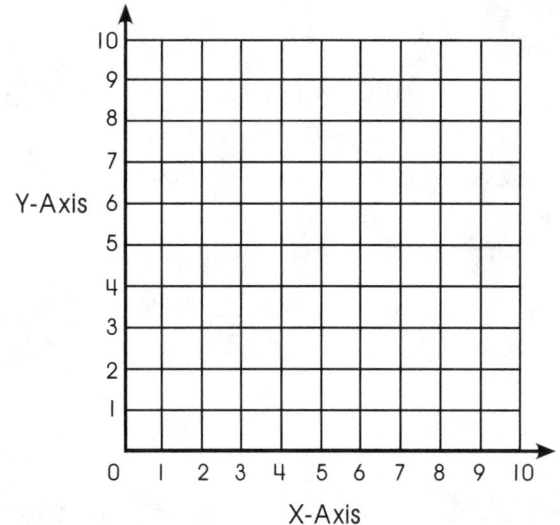

What kind of polygon is made? _____

2. (3, 4)

(3, 8)

(5, 4)

(5, 8)

(2, 6)

(6, 6)

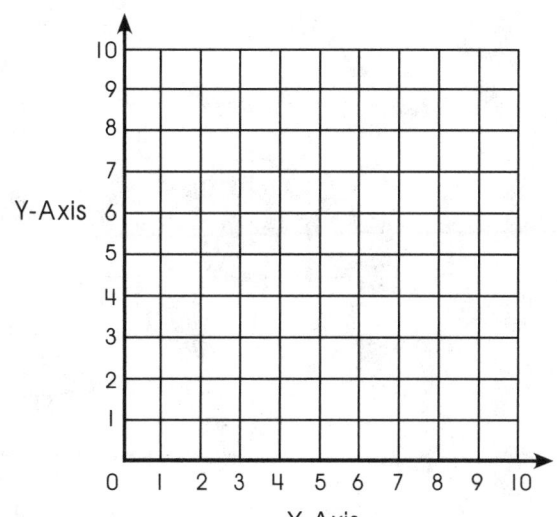

What kind of polygon is made? _____

3. Find all of the possible lines of symmetry on the polygon in problem number two. Draw the lines on the figure.

Name: _____   Date: _____

My Neighborhood   Coordinate Graphing

Use ordered pairs to name the locations on the grid.

1. Tyler's house is located at (_____ , _____) on the grid.

2. The school is located at (_____ , _____) on the grid.

3. Find the fewest number of blocks Tyler must walk to get to Zachary's house. Think of the lines of the grid as streets. Tyler can only travel on the lines of the grid. He may not travel on any diagonal lines.

_____ blocks

4. Thea's house is located at (2,4) on the grid. Put an X where Thea's house is located.

5. Zachary's house is five blocks from the school. How many different five-block paths can Zachary walk on his way to school?

_____ paths

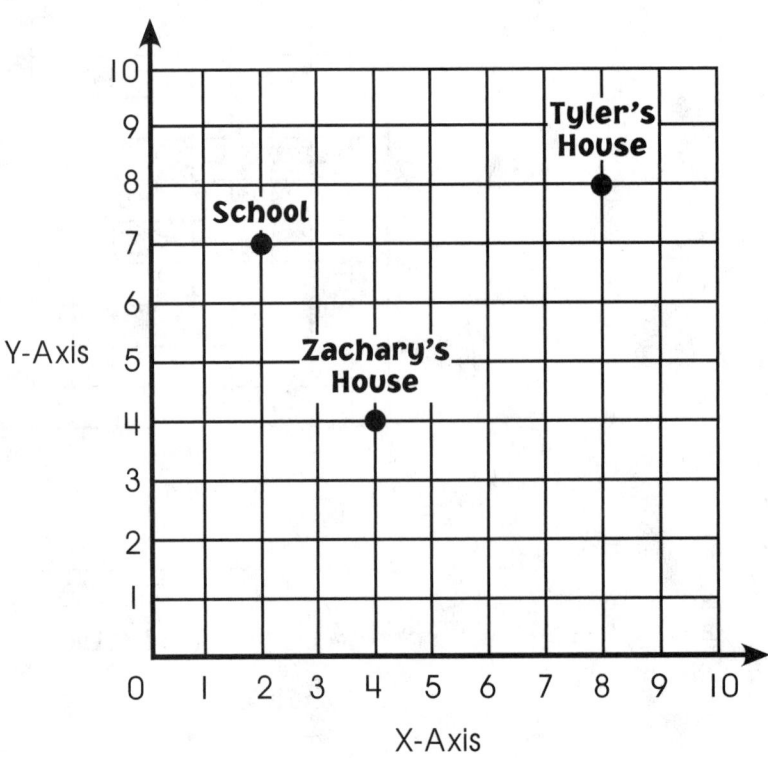

Name: _____ Date: _____

Favorite Places — Coordinate Graphing

Locate the following places on the grid below and record the coordinates.

		x	y			x	y
1.	zoo	(_____ , _____)		**2.**	playground	(_____ , _____)	
3.	swimming pool	(_____ , _____)		**4.**	candy store	(_____ , _____)	
5.	school	(_____ , _____)		**6.**	friend's house	(_____ , _____)	
7.	lake	(_____ , _____)		**8.**	amusement park	(_____ , _____)	
9.	grocery store	(_____ , _____)		**10.**	beach	(_____ , _____)	
11.	campground	(_____ , _____)		**12.**	skating rink	(_____ , _____)	
13.	public library	(_____ , _____)		**14.**	grandparents' house	(_____ , _____)	

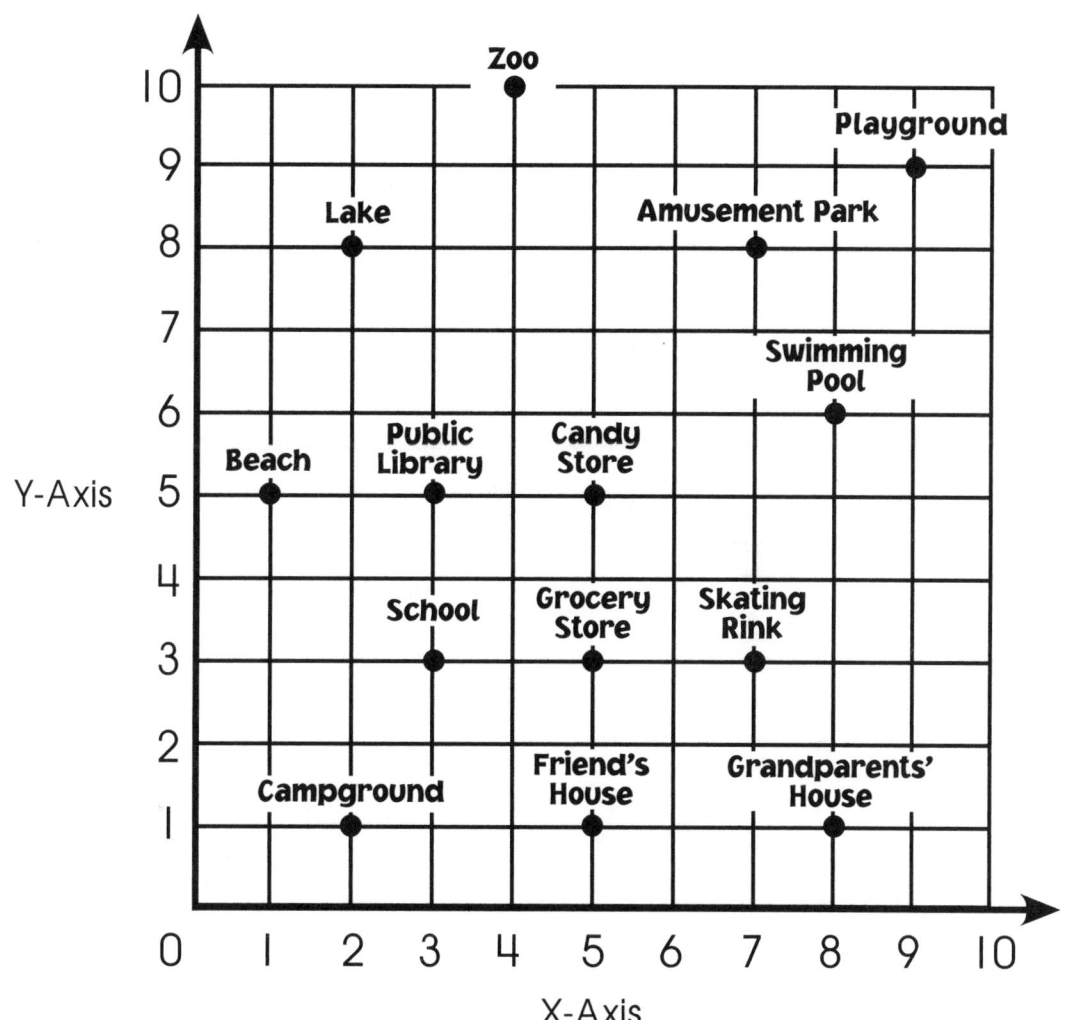

Toy Store Hunt

Coordinate Graphing

Use the ordered pairs listed below to locate the items in the toy store. Remember to begin with at the x-axis. Write what type of toy is at each location.

(x, y)

1. (7, 3) _____

3. (3, 4) _____

5. (2, 7) _____

7. (6, 2) _____

9. (1, 10) _____

11. (9, 9) _____

(x, y)

2. (5, 8) _____

4. (8, 1) _____

6. (4, 2) _____

8. (6, 9) _____

10. (3, 9) _____

12. (1, 2) _____

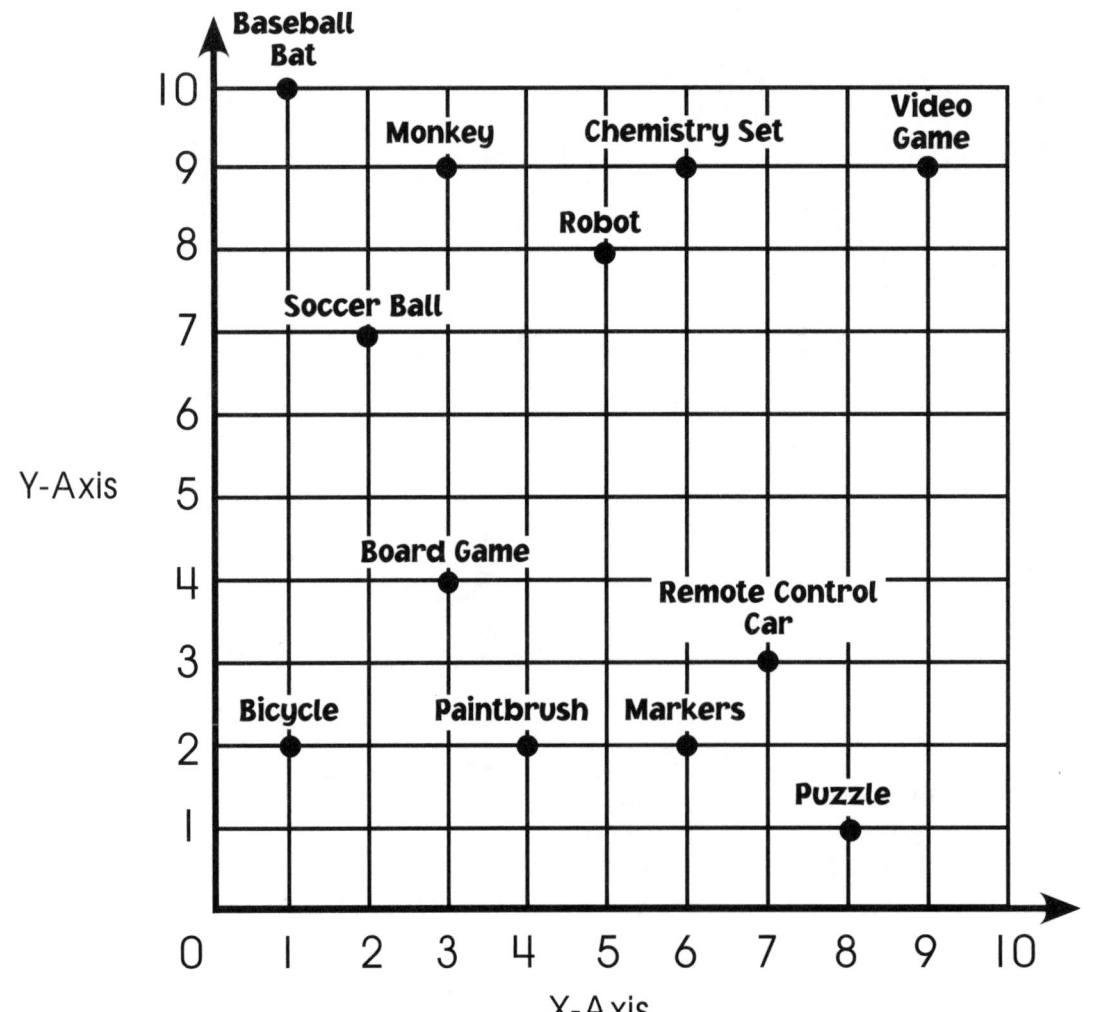

Name: _____   Date: _____

Coordinate Graphing Riddle   Coordinate Graphing

Read the ordered pairs and find the points on the grid below. Write the letters on the blanks to answer the riddle.

Riddle: What do you get when you cross geometry with a hamburger stand?

Answer:

___ " ___ ___ ___ ___ ___ "
(5, 8)   (2, 5) (8, 7) (5, 8) (7, 4) (1, 2)

___ ___ ___ ___ ___ ___ ___ ___ ___ ___ ___ ___
(2, 9) (9, 1) (1, 2) (1, 2) (5, 6) (1, 2) (7, 9) (3, 4) (6, 1) (1, 7) (1, 2) (6, 1)

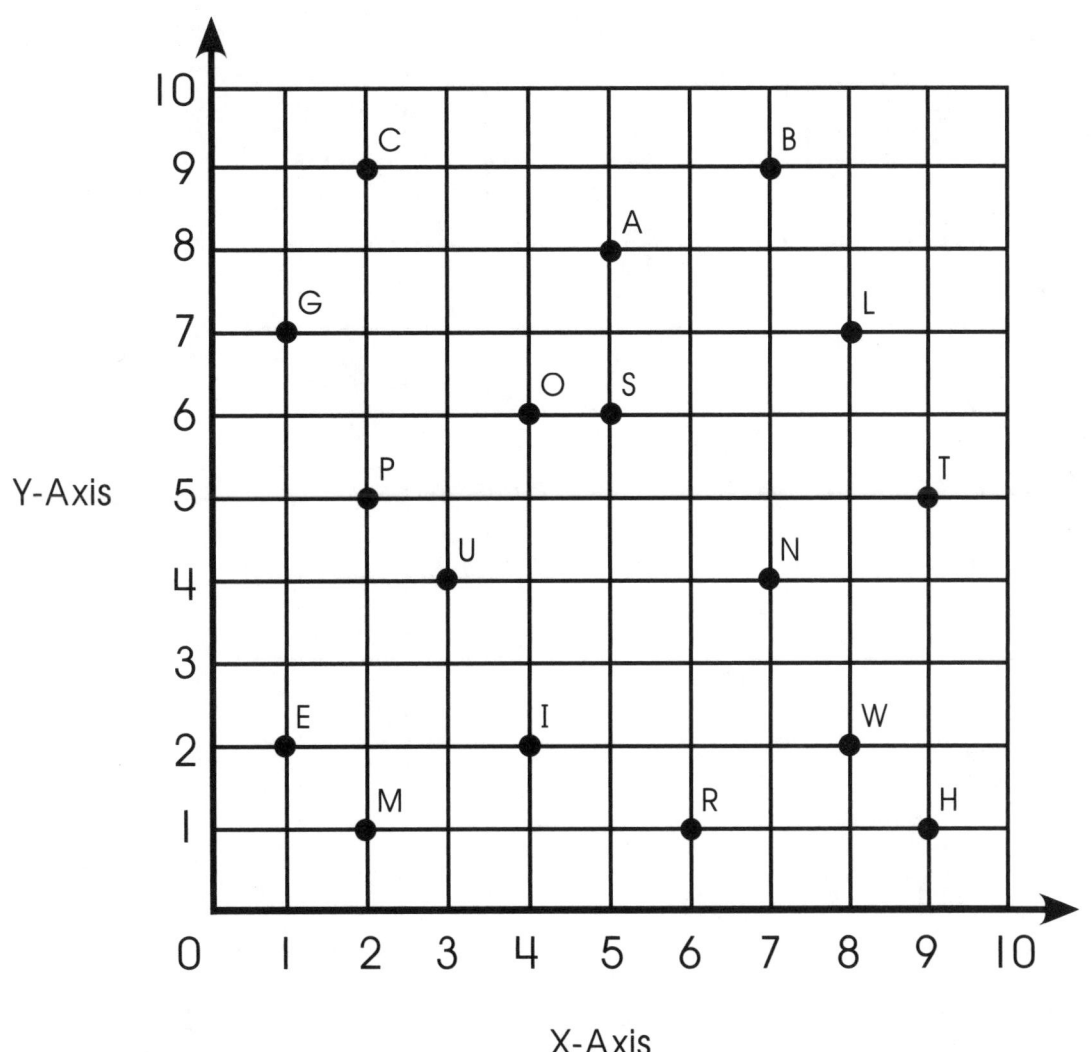

Name: _____   Date: _____

Draw the coordinate points on the grid below. Connect them in the order given.

1. (2, 2) ⟶ (3, 2) ⟶ (4, 2) ⟶ (4, 3) ⟶ (4, 4) ⟶ (5, 4) ⟶ (5, 3) ⟶ (5, 2) ⟶
   (6, 2) ⟶ (7, 2) ⟶ (8, 2) ⟶ (8, 3) ⟶ (8, 4) ⟶ (8, 5) ⟶ (9, 5) ⟶ (8, 6) ⟶
   (7, 7) ⟶ (6, 8) ⟶ (5, 9) ⟶ (4, 8) ⟶ (3, 7) ⟶ (3, 8) ⟶ (3, 9) ⟶ (2, 9) ⟶
   (2, 8) ⟶ (2, 7) ⟶ (2, 6) ⟶ (1, 5) ⟶ (2, 5) ⟶ (2, 4) ⟶ (2, 3) ⟶ (2,2)

   What figure did you create? _____

2. Now, color and decorate your drawing!

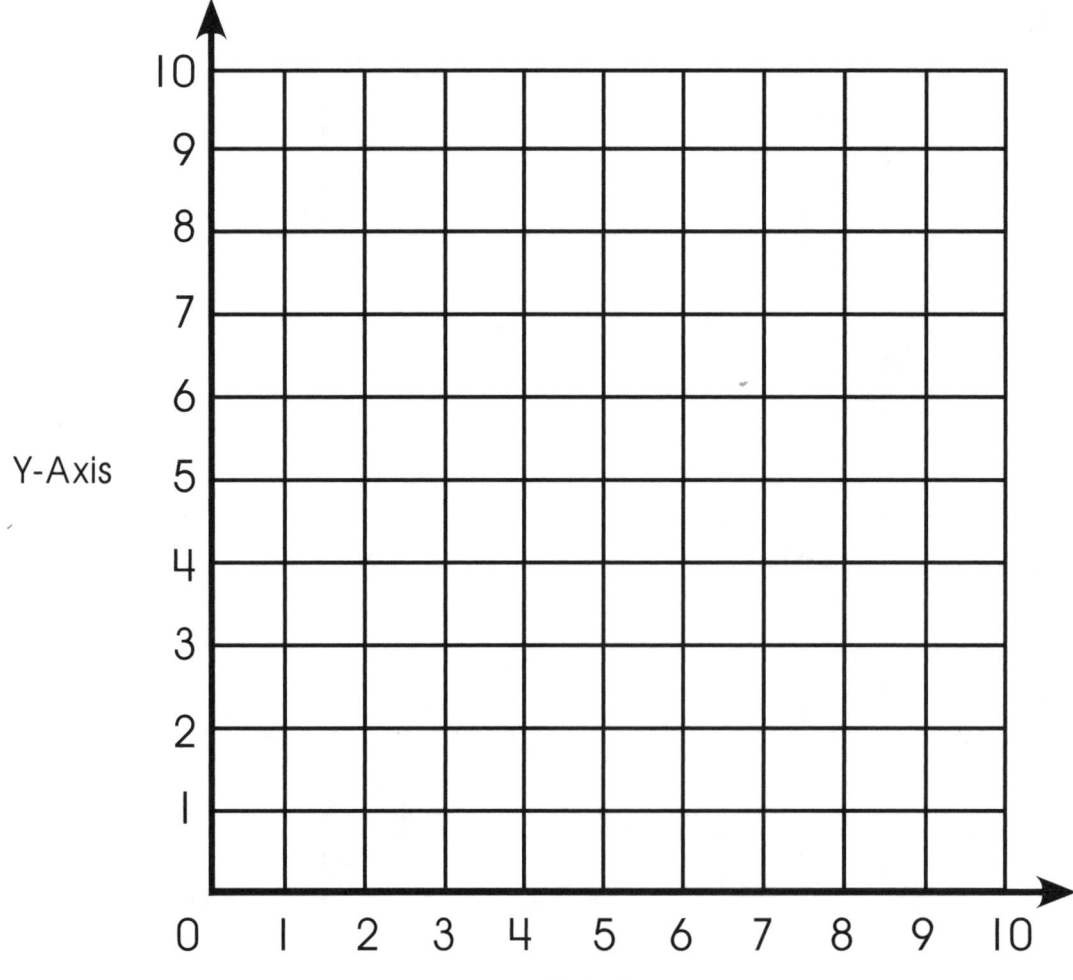

Symmetrical Graphing

Coordinate Graphing

Draw the coordinate points on the grid below. Connect in the order given. Then, draw the mirror image on the right side of the dark line to complete the figure.

(5, 0) ⟶ (4, 1) ⟶ (3, 2) ⟶ (2, 3) ⟶ (3, 3) ⟶ (4, 3) ⟶ (4, 4) ⟶ (4, 5) ⟶
(4, 6) ⟶ (4, 7) ⟶ (3, 7) ⟶ (2, 7) ⟶ (3, 8) ⟶ (4, 9) ⟶ (5, 10)

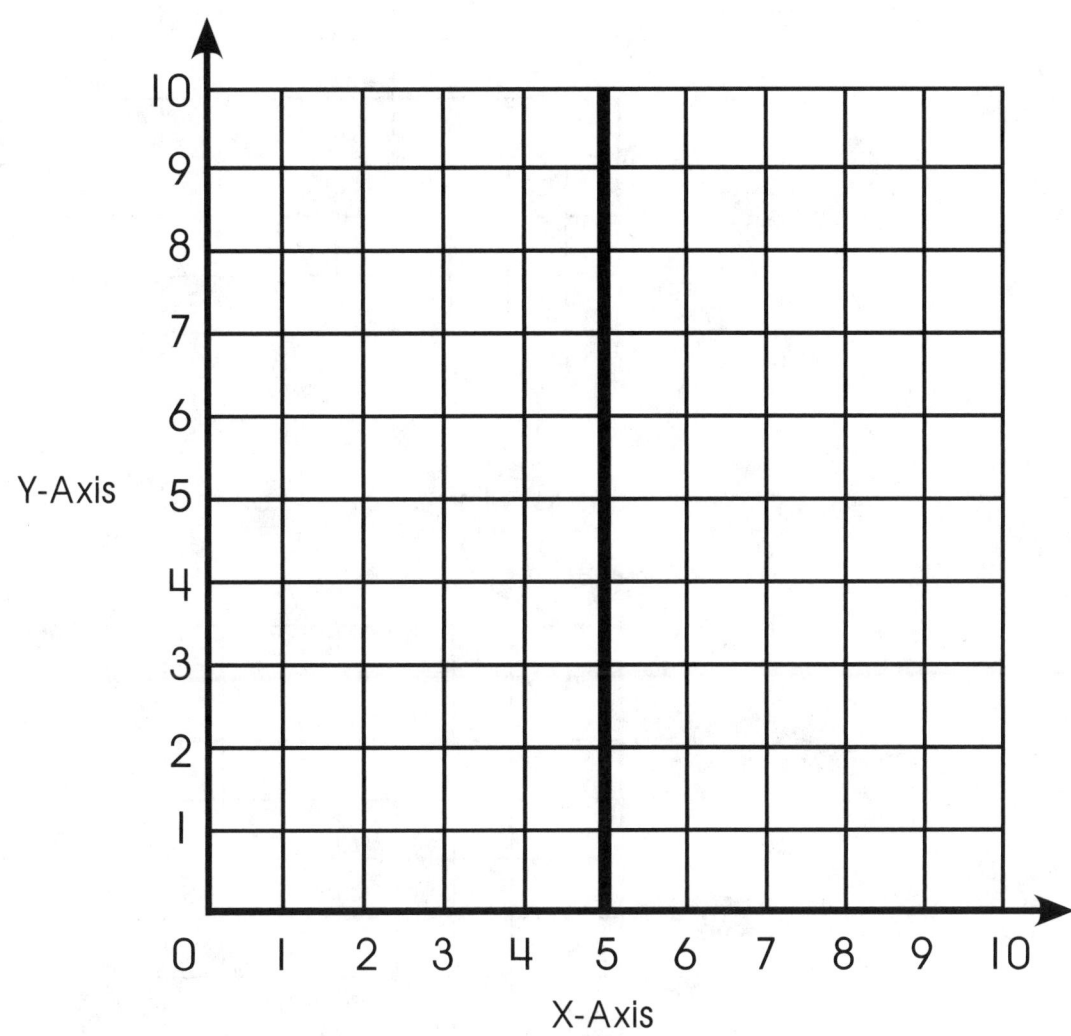

Y-Axis

X-Axis

Name: _____   Date: _____

Identify the ordered pair for each point. Write the numbers for x and y.

1. U (____ , ____)

2. V (____ , ____)

3. W (____ , ____)

4. X (____ , ____)

5. Y (____ , ____)

6. Z (____ , ____)

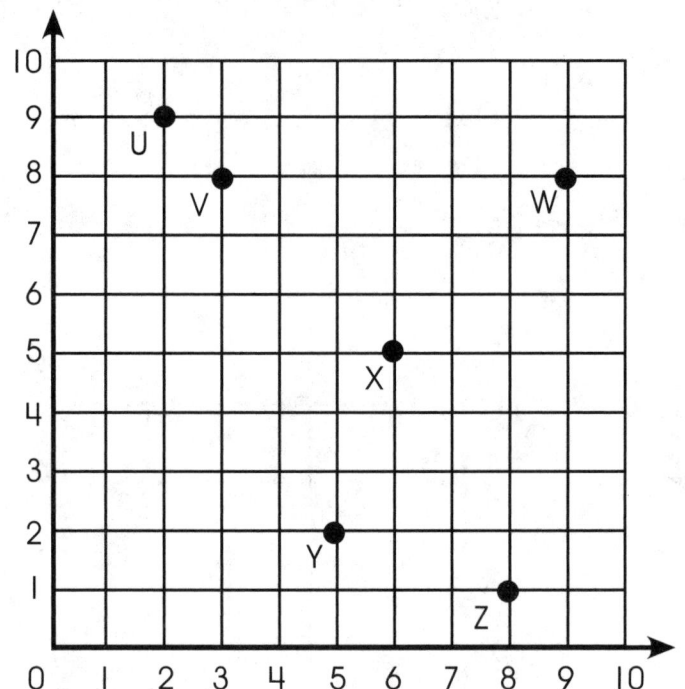

Plot the following ordered pairs by drawing and labeling the points on the coordinate grid.

7. A (6, 0)

8. B (2, 2)

9. C (4, 3)

10. D (10, 4)

11. E (8, 3)

12. F (0, 0)

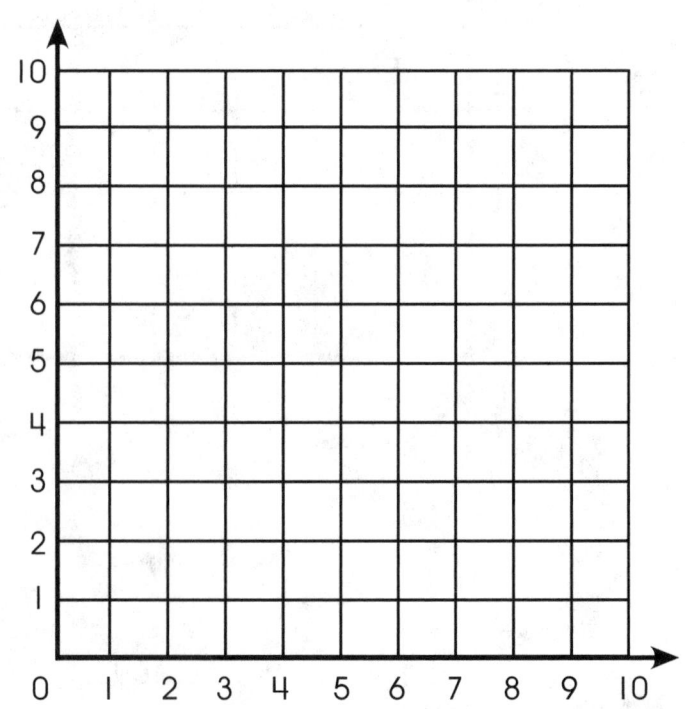

Coordinate Graphing: Mixed Review 2   Coordinate Graphing

Plot the following ordered pairs by drawing and labeling the points on the coordinate grid.

1. N (1, 1)
2. O (2, 2)
3. P (3, 3)
4. Q (4, 4)
5. R (5, 5)
6. S (6, 6)

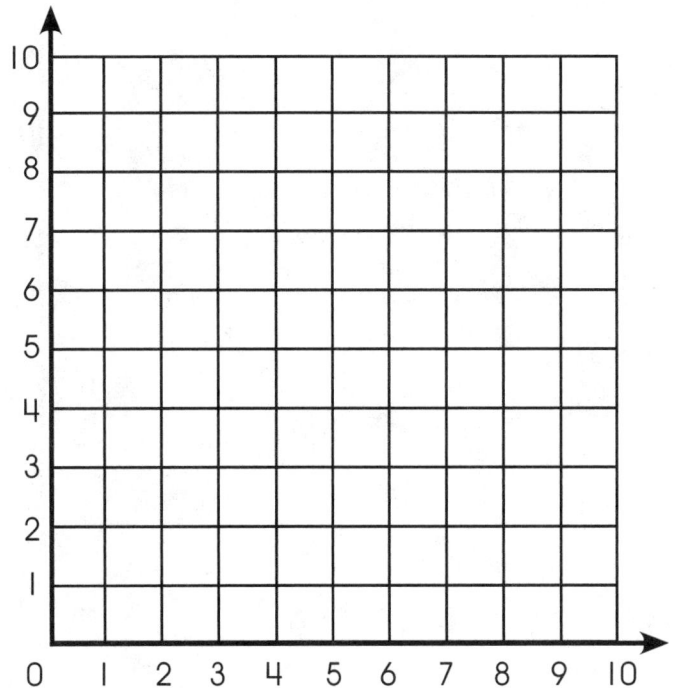

Identify the ordered pair for each point. Write the numbers for x and y.

1. H (____ , ____)
2. I (____ , ____)
3. J (____ , ____)
4. K (____ , ____)
5. L (____ , ____)
6. M (____ , ____)

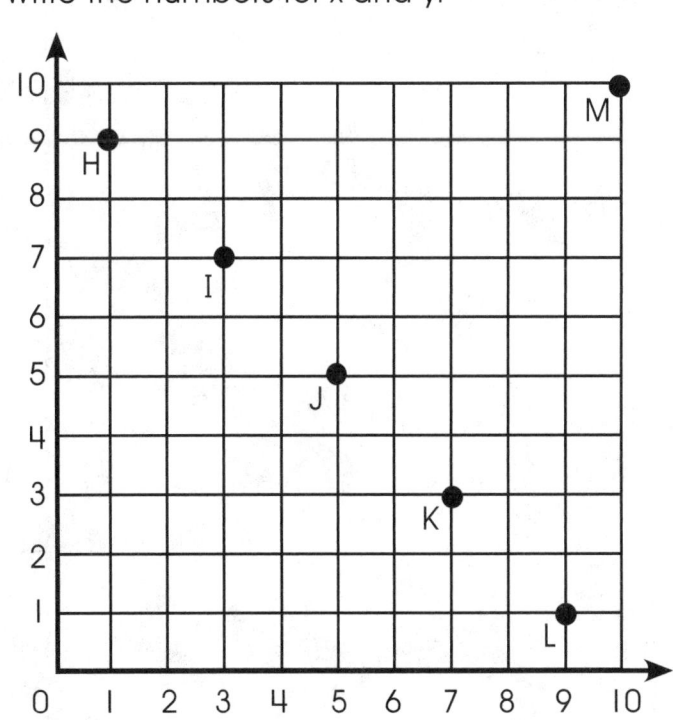

Name: _____ Date: _____

Identify the ordered pair for each point. Write the numbers for x and y.

1. A (____ , ____)

2. C (____ , ____)

3. E (____ , ____)

4. G (____ , ____)

5. I (____ , ____)

6. K (____ , ____)

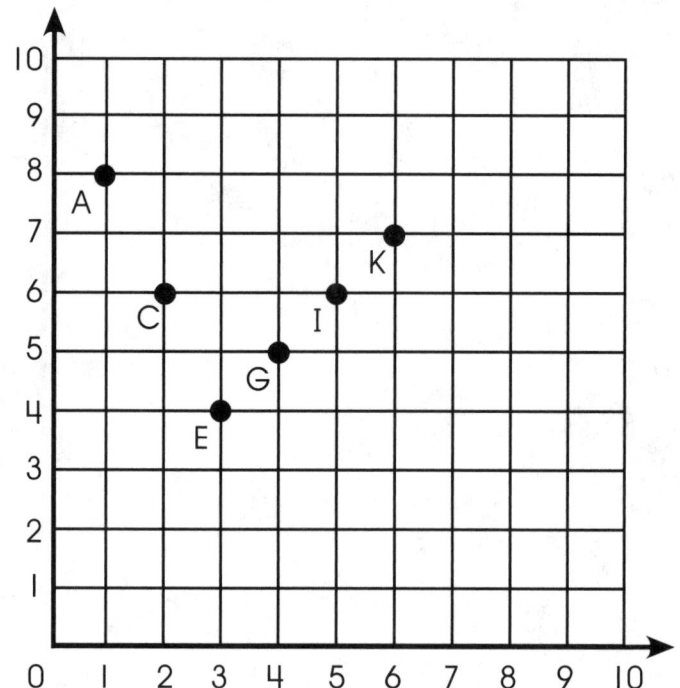

Plot the following ordered pairs by drawing and labeling the points on the coordinate grid.

7. R (1, 1)

8. S (7, 4)

9. T (5, 2)

10. U (2, 5)

11. V (8, 2)

12. W (10, 0)

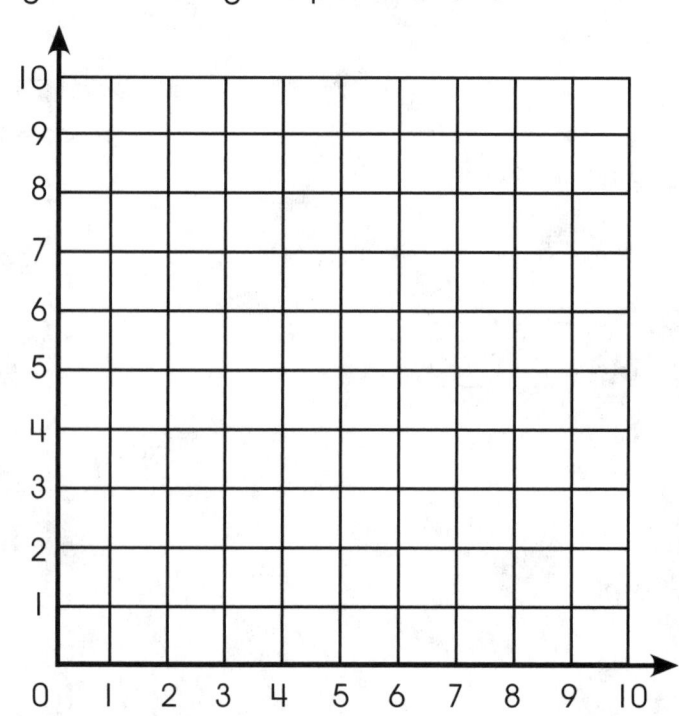

Final Review   Page 1

1. Circle the lines that are perpendicular.

A.    B.

C. 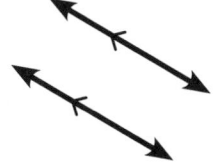   D.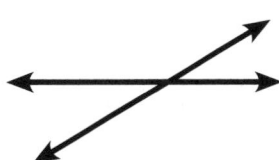

2. Identify the angle to the right and circle its name.

A. acute

B. right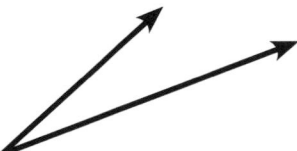

C. obtuse

3. An angle measuring 90° is classified as what type of angle? _____

Draw and label the following.

4. acute angle XYZ   **5.** obtuse angle ABC   **6.** right angle EFG

7. line segment OP   **8.** ray LM   **9.** line JK

Final Review

10. Use a protractor to measure angle ABC. Circle the measurement below.

A. 44°   B. 27°   C. 75°   D. 82°

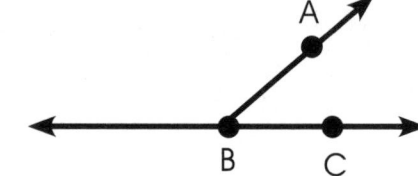

11. Circle the name of the polygon that has five sides.

A. quadrilateral   B. hexagon   C. pentagon   D. octagon

Match each figure with the correct name in the box. Write the letter for the name.

12. _____

13. _____

14. _____

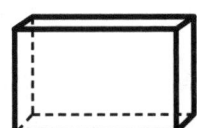

A. octagon

B. trapezoid

C. rectangular prism

D. triangle

E. quadrilateral

F. hexagon

Name a polygon that has exactly:

15. one right angle _____

16. two right angles _____

17. four right angles _____

Name: _____ Date: _____

Final Review

Page 3

Use the terms in the box to complete the following statements.

18. A circle contains _____ degrees.	coordinate
19. When thinking about circumference, remember _____.	angles
20. The area of a rectangle is length times _____.	180
21. Every triangle contains _____ degrees.	pi
22. Points are located on a _____ grid.	perimeter
23. A _____ triangle has one right angle.	width
24. The _____ of a triangle is the sum of the lengths of its sides.	height
25. The area of a triangle is _____ times base divided by two.	360
	right

coordinate
angles
180
pi
perimeter
width
height
360
right

26. In geometry, the terms *right*, *obtuse* and *acute* refer to _____ .

Write the names of the following figures.

27.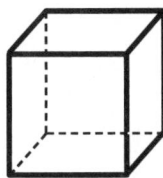

28.

29.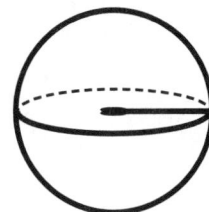

_____

_____

_____

30. Find the radius.

16 cm

31. Find the diameter.

26 in.

32. Find the circumference using pi.

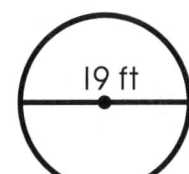
19 ft

_____

_____

_____

Name: _____ Date: _____

Answer the following questions.

33. Is a diameter also a chord? Explain. _____

_____

34. The radius of circle one is 18 inches. The diameter of circle two is 36 inches. Which

circle is bigger? _____

35. Three angles of a quadrilateral measure 92°, 143°, and 31°. What does the fourth
angle measure?

A. 277°   B. 77°   C. 94°   D. 134°

36. Write *true* or *false*: All angles in a regular octagon are acute. _____

37. Circle the triangle below that has two sides measuring the same length and an
interior angle measuring 100°.

A. acute scalene   B. obtuse isosceles   C. acute isosceles   D. obtuse scalene

38. What is the name of a three-sided polygon with three unequal side lengths?

_____

34. Can a triangle have two right angles? Explain. _____

_____

Look at the figures to the right. Circle the correct answers.

40. A. These are both rectangles.

B. These are congruent figures.

C. These are not congruent figures.

D. none of the above

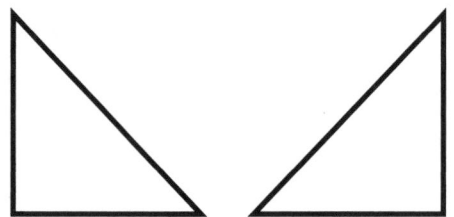

41. A. These are similar figures.

B. These are congruent figures.

C. These are not congruent figures.

D. none of the above

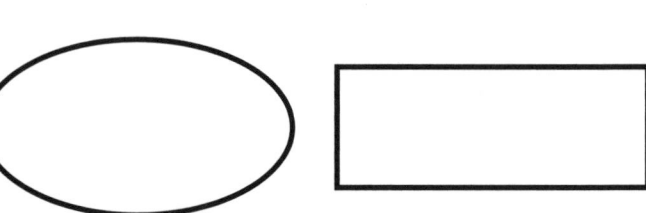

Determine how each figure was moved. Write *flip*, *slide*, or *turn*.

42.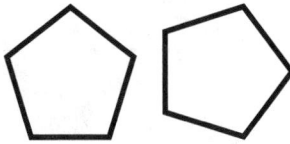

43.

44.

_____   _____   _____

45. How many lines of symmetry does this figure have?
Draw them and write the number below.

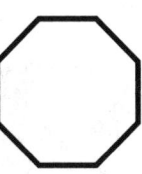

_____

Circle the correct answers.

46. A square piece of poster board has a perimeter of 12 centimeters. What is the area of the poster board?

A. 144 square centimeters   B. 9 square centimeters

C. 16 square centimeters   D. 24 square centimeters

47. A parallelogram is 5 inches wide. The area of the parallelogram is 35 square inches. What is the perimeter of the parallelogram?

A. 24 inches   B. 40 inches   C. 30 inches   D. There is not enough information to know.

48. Tyler's room is exactly 18 feet by 21 feet. He wants to get carpeting to cover the entire floor. How many square yards of carpeting does he need?

A. 126   B. 378   C. 13   D. 42

Find the area and perimeter of each of the following figures.

49.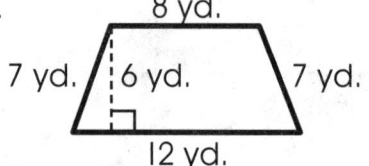

A = _____

P = _____

50.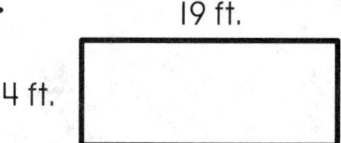

A = _____

P = _____

51.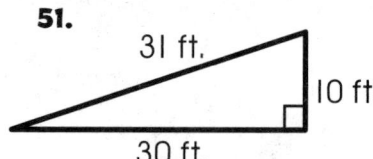

A = _____

P = _____

Find the volume of each of the following figures.

52.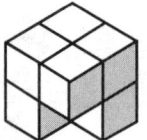

V = _____

53.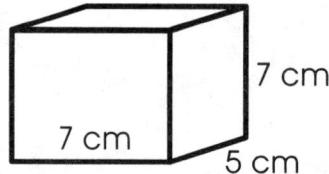

V = _____

54.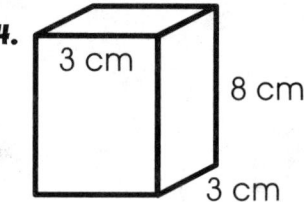

V = _____

Plot the following ordered pairs by drawing and labeling the points on the coordinate grid.

55. A (3, 0)

56. B (6, 8)

57. C (4, 10)

58. D (2, 9)

59. E (1, 3)

60. F (9, 6)

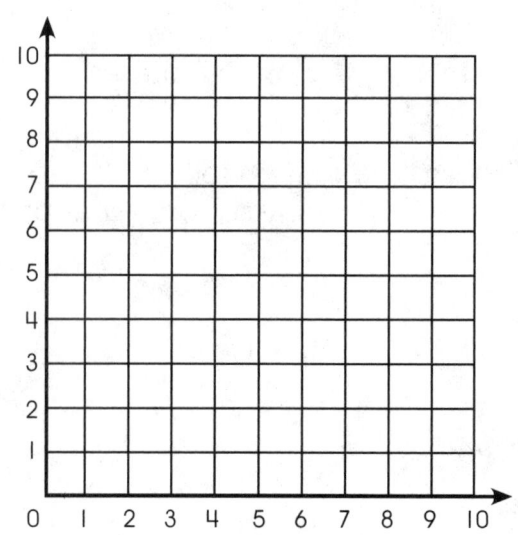

Formulas

Area of a Parallelogram $A = bh$

The area of a parallelogram is computed by multiplying the base by the height.

Area of a Rectangle $A = lw$

The area of a rectangle is computed by multiplying the width of one side by the length of the adjoining side. The area of a rectangle can also be found by multiplying the base by the height.

Area of a Square $A = s^2$ OR $A = s \cdot s$

A square is a special rectangle. The area of a square is computed by using the rectangle formula. However, since all of the sides are the same length, the measurement of one side can be squared to find the area.

Area of a Trapezoid $A = \frac{1}{2}h(b_1 + b_2)$

To find the area of a trapezoid, draw a diagonal so that the trapezoid is cut into two triangles. Find the area of each triangle. Then, add the two triangles together to find the area of the trapezoid.

Area of a Triangle $A = \frac{1}{2}bh$

A triangle is always one-half of a rectangle or a parallelogram. The area of a triangle is computed by multiplying one-half of the base by the height.

Circumference $C = \pi d$ OR $C = 2\pi r$

The circumference is the distance around a circle. To find the circumference of a circle, multiply π (which always equals approximately 3.14) by the diameter. Or, multiply two times π (3.14) by the radius.

Diameter $d = 2r$

Diameter is the distance from one side of a circle to the other passing through the circle's center. To find the diameter of a circle multiply the radius of the circle times two.

Perimeter $P = (2 \cdot l) + (2 \cdot w)$

Perimeter is the length around a closed figure. It is computed by finding the total length of all of the sides of the figure.

Radius $r = d/2$

The radius is the line segment, or distance, from the center of a circle to a point on the circle. To find the radius of a circle, divide the diameter of the circle by two.

Volume $V = lwh$

To find the volume of a rectangular prism, such as a box, multiply the length by the width by the height.

Glossary of Geometric Terms

acute angle—an angle that measures more than 0 degrees but less than 90 degrees (page 11)

acute triangle—a triangle with three acute angles (or no angle measuring 90 degrees or greater) (page 21)

angle—two rays that share an endpoint (page 11)

Area—the number of square units enclosed within a boundary; area is measured in square units such as square feet or square centimeters (pages 54, 56)

center—the center point of a circle or sphere naming the circle or sphere (pages 33, 37)

chord—a line segment passing through a circle that has its endpoints on that circle (pages 33, 37)

circle—a closed curve with all points in one plane and equidistant from a fixed point (the center) (page 33)

circumference—the distance around a circle; circumference can be computed by multiplying the diameter by pi (π), a number a little more than 3.14 (pages 70, 71)

cone—a solid figure with a circular base joined to a vertex by a curved surface (page 43)

congruent—having exactly the same size and shape (pages 19, 73)

coordinate grid—a reference system for locating and graphing points; in two dimensions, a coordinate grid usually consists of a horizontal axis and a vertical axis, which intersect at the origin; these distances, or coordinates, form an ordered pair of numbers (page 92)

cube—a solid figure in which every face is a square and every edge is the same length (page 42)

cylinder—a solid figure formed by two congruent parallel circles joined by a curved surface (page 43)

diameter—a line segment passing through the center of a circle or sphere and connecting two points on the circle or sphere (pages 33, 34, 35)

edge—a line segment where two faces of a solid figure meet (page 41)

endpoint—the point(s) at the end of a ray or line segment (page 7)

equiangular triangle—a triangle with three congruent angles; each angle measures 60 degrees (page 21)

equilateral triangle—a triangle with three congruent sides; each angle measures 60 degrees (page 19)

face—a plane figure that serves as one side of a solid figure (page 41)

flip—a transformation of a geometric figure that results in a mirror image of the original (page 84)

hexagon—a polygon with six sides; a regular hexagon has six congruent sides and six congruent angles (page 29)

intersecting lines—lines that cross each other at only one point (page 9)

isosceles triangle—a triangle with at least two congruent sides and two congruent angles (page 19)

line—a set of points that form a straight path extending infinitely in two directions (page 6)

line of symmetry—a line dividing a two-dimensional figure into two parts that are mirror images of each other; a figure that contains such a line has line symmetry (pages 76, 77, 81)

line segment—a part of a line; a line segment has two endpoints and a finite length (page 7)

net—a diagram showing all of the faces of a solid figure as if it were unfolded (page 44)

noncollinear—points not on the same line (page 14)

obtuse angle—an angle that measures more than 90 degrees but less than 180 degrees (page 11)

obtuse triangle—a triangle that has one obtuse angle (page 21)

octagon—a polygon with eight sides; a regular octagon has eight congruent sides and eight congruent angles (page 29)

ordered pair—a set of coordinates (x, y) in a coordinate grid

parallel lines—lines in the same plane that are always the same distance apart and never intersect (page 9)

parallelogram—a quadrilateral with both pairs of opposite sides parallel; opposite sides and angles are congruent (page 27)

pentagon—a polygon with five sides; a regular pentagon has five congruent sides and five congruent angles (page 29)

perimeter—the distance around a figure (page 50)

perpendicular lines—lines that intersect to form right angles (page 9)

plane—a flat surface extending infinitely in all directions (page 14)

point—the smallest geometric unit; a position in space, often represented by a dot (page 6)

point of intersection—the point at which two lines cross (page 9)

Glossary of Geometric Terms

polygon—a simple, closed plane figure created by three or more straight line segments connected so that the area is closed in (page 17)

prism—a solid figure in which two faces are polygons in parallel planes and the other faces are parallelograms (page 42)

pyramid—a solid figure in which the base is a polygon and the faces are triangles with a common vertex (page 42)

quadrilateral—a polygon with four sides (page 18)

radius—a line segment with one endpoint at the center of a circle and the other endpoint on that circle (pages 33, 34, 35)

ray—a set of points that forms a straight path extending infinitely in one direction; a ray has one endpoint (page 7)

rectangle—a parallelogram with four right angles; opposite sides are congruent and parallel (page 27)

rectangular prism—a solid figure in which all six faces are rectangles with three pairs of opposite faces that are parallel and congruent (page 42)

regular polygon—a polygon that has equal sides and equal angles

regular tessellation—an arrangement of regular polygons that are all the same; each vertex must look the same (page 90)

rhombus—a parallelogram with four congruent sides; opposite angles are congruent, and opposite sides are parallel (page 27)

right angle—an angle that measures 90 degrees (page 11)

right triangle—a triangle that has one right angle (page 21)

scalene triangle—a triangle with no congruent sides (page 19)

similar—figures that have the same shape but not necessarily the same size (page 74)

slide—a transformation in which a geometric figure is formed by moving every point on a figure the same distance in the same direction (page 84)

solid—a closed, three-dimensional figure that contains edges, faces, and vertices (page 41)

sphere—a solid figure formed by a set of points that are all the same distance from a fixed point called the center (page 43)

square—a rectangle with four congruent sides; opposite sides are parallel (page 27)

square unit—a unit of measure that has a length of one unit and a width of one unit; used to measure area; examples are square inches, square centimeters, etc. (page 54)

---

symmetrical—when a figure can be folded along a line so that the two halves are mirror images, the two sides of the figure are symmetrical (page 76)

tessellation—an arrangement of plane figures (possibly a combination of figures like hexagons and triangles) to cover a surface without overlapping or leaving any gaps (page 90)

three-dimensional—relating to objects that have length, width, and depth; solid figures, such as cones and spheres, are three-dimensional (page 41)

transformation—moving a geometric figure from one position to another, according to a rule; examples of transformations are turns, slides, and flips (page 84)

trapezoid—a quadrilateral with exactly one pair of parallel sides (page 27)

triangle—a polygon with three sides (pages 19, 21)

triangular prism—a prism in which the base is a rectangle (page 42)

triangular pyramid—a pyramid in which all sides are triangles (page 42)

turn—a transformation in which a geometric figure is rotated around a fixed point (page 84)

Venn diagram—a diagram that uses overlapping circles to show elements and what they have in common (page 47)

vertex—a point at which two line segments, lines, or rays meet to form an angle; also, a point on a solid figure where three or more faces meet; the plural of vertex is vertices (pages 13, 41)

volume—an amount of space within a solid figure measured in cubic units (page 66)

x-axis—the horizontal axis in a coordinate grid (page 92)

y-axis—the vertical axis in a plane coordinate grid (page 92)

Answer Key

Page 6

1. line AB; 2. points V and W; 3. point T; 4. line XZ; 5. line CD; 6. line WX; 7. line JK; 8. points R, V, and O

Page 7

1. ray XY; 2. line segment DE; 3. points S and T; 4. line WX; 5. line CD; 6. points H, I, and J; 7. line segment JK; 8. ray LM

Page 8

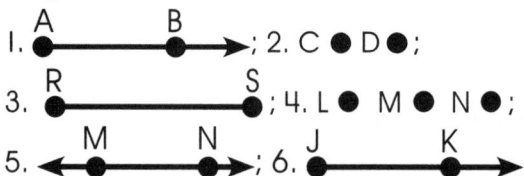

7. L, M, N, O; 8. Answers will vary but may include $\overline{LM}$, $\overline{MN}$, $\overline{OM}$, $\overline{LN}$; 9. LM, LN, MN; 10. Answers will vary but may include $\overrightarrow{ML}$, $\overrightarrow{LN}$, $\overrightarrow{MO}$, $\overrightarrow{ML}$, $\overrightarrow{MN}$, $\overrightarrow{NM}$, $\overrightarrow{NL}$; 11. Answers will vary but may include X, Y, Z, V, W; 12. Answers will vary but may include $\overleftrightarrow{XW}$, $\overleftrightarrow{XY}$, $\overleftrightarrow{YW}$, $\overleftrightarrow{VY}$, $\overleftrightarrow{YZ}$, $\overleftrightarrow{VZ}$; 13. Answers will vary but may include $\overline{YX}$, $\overline{VZ}$, $\overline{YW}$, $\overline{ZY}$, $\overline{VY}$, $\overline{XW}$; 14. Answers will vary but may include $\overrightarrow{YX}$, $\overrightarrow{YV}$, $\overrightarrow{YW}$, $\overrightarrow{YZ}$, $\overrightarrow{ZV}$, $\overrightarrow{XW}$, $\overrightarrow{VZ}$, $\overrightarrow{WX}$

Page 9

1. point S; 2. 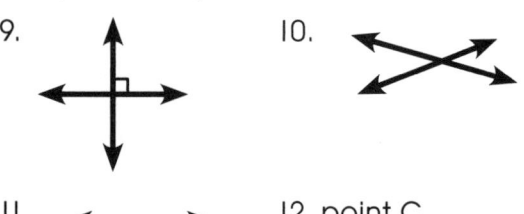 3. ; 4. perpendicular; 5. neither; 6. parallel

Page 10

1. line segment TU; 2. line segment XY; 3. ray MN; 4. line segment RP; 5. line AB; 6. line FG; 7. ray CE; 8. ray NM;

9. 10. 11. 12. point C

13. Answers will vary but may include $\overleftrightarrow{ZE}$, $\overleftrightarrow{ZC}$, $\overleftrightarrow{CE}$, $\overleftrightarrow{DC}$, $\overleftrightarrow{CB}$, $\overleftrightarrow{DB}$; 14. Answers will vary but may

include $\overline{CZ}$, $\overline{CE}$, $\overline{ZE}$, $\overline{DB}$, $\overline{DC}$, $\overline{CB}$; 15. Answers will vary but may include $\overrightarrow{CZ}$, $\overrightarrow{CD}$, $\overrightarrow{CE}$, $\overrightarrow{CB}$, $\overrightarrow{EZ}$, $\overrightarrow{DB}$, $\overrightarrow{ZE}$, $\overrightarrow{BD}$

Page 11

1. obtuse; 2. right; 3. acute; 4. acute; 5. right; 6. right; 7. right; 8. acute; 9. acute; 10. obtuse; 11. right; 12. acute

Page 12

1.–3. Answers will vary; 4. acute; 5. right; 6. obtuse; 7. right; 8. right; 9. acute; 10. right; 11. right; 12. acute; 13. acute; 14. right; 15. acute

Page 13

1. 160°, obtuse; 2. 95°, obtuse; 3. 130°, obtuse; 4. 40°, acute; 5. 90°, right; 6. 70°, acute

Page 14

1.
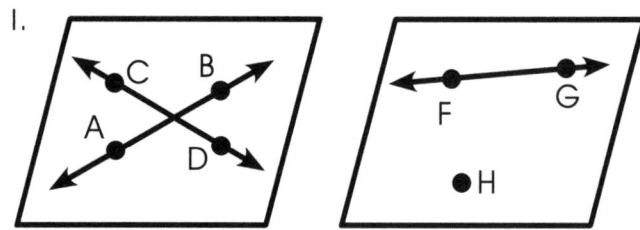

2. Answers will vary but must include three noncollinear points; 3. Answers will vary

Page 15

1. $\overleftrightarrow{AC}$ and $\overleftrightarrow{DF}$; 2. Answers will vary but may include ∠ABG, ∠DEH, ∠IEF, ∠CBL, ∠KBL, ∠KBG, ∠BEH; 3. ∠ABK, ∠KBC, ∠BED, ∠ABE, ∠EBC, ∠BEF, ∠DEM, ∠MEF; 4. Answers will vary but may include ∠ABL, ∠GBC, ∠HEF, ∠EBL, ∠MEH, ∠EBG; 5. acute; 6. right; 7. $\overleftrightarrow{AC}$ and $\overleftrightarrow{DF}$; 8. Answers will vary but may include $\overleftrightarrow{HI}$ and $\overleftrightarrow{DF}$, $\overleftrightarrow{BE}$ and $\overleftrightarrow{DF}$, $\overleftrightarrow{AC}$ and $\overleftrightarrow{BE}$; 9. Answers will vary but may include M, L, T, W, K, S, R, U; 10. Answers will vary but may include $\overleftrightarrow{ML}$, $\overleftrightarrow{MT}$, $\overleftrightarrow{MW}$, $\overleftrightarrow{KU}$, $\overleftrightarrow{KL}$, $\overleftrightarrow{LU}$, $\overleftrightarrow{RU}$, $\overleftrightarrow{RS}$, $\overleftrightarrow{RT}$, $\overleftrightarrow{ST}$; 11. $\overleftrightarrow{MW}$ and $\overleftrightarrow{RU}$; 12. Answers will vary but may include $\overline{ML}$, $\overline{LT}$, $\overline{TW}$, $\overline{KL}$, $\overline{LU}$, $\overline{RS}$, $\overline{ST}$, $\overline{TU}$, $\overline{SW}$; 13. $\overleftrightarrow{SW}$ and $\overleftrightarrow{KU}$;

Answer Key

14. Answers will vary but may include $\overrightarrow{LM}$, $\overrightarrow{LU}$, $\overrightarrow{LK}$, $\overrightarrow{TM}$, $\overrightarrow{TW}$, $\overrightarrow{SW}$, $\overrightarrow{SR}$, $\overrightarrow{TU}$, $\overrightarrow{WS}$

Page 16

1. Answers will vary but may include A, B, C, D, E, F, G, H 2. Answers will vary but may include $\overline{DB}$, $\overline{FH}$, $\overline{AB}$, $\overline{BC}$, $\overline{EF}$, $\overline{FG}$, $\overline{EG}$, $\overline{AC}$, $\overline{DH}$, $\overline{BF}$; 3. Answers will vary but may include $\overrightarrow{BD}$, $\overrightarrow{AB}$, $\overleftrightarrow{BC}$, $\overleftrightarrow{FE}$, $\overleftrightarrow{FG}$, $\overleftrightarrow{FH}$; 4. $\overleftrightarrow{DH}$ and $\overleftrightarrow{EG}$; 5. D, B, F, H; 6. no parallel lines; 7. $\overleftrightarrow{AC}$ and $\overleftrightarrow{DH}$ or $\overleftrightarrow{EG}$ and $\overleftrightarrow{DH}$; 8. Answers will vary but may include ∠ABD, ∠CBD, ∠ABF, ∠EFB, ∠EFH, ∠EFG, ∠GFH, ∠CBF, ∠GFB; 9. $\overleftrightarrow{AC}$ and $\overleftrightarrow{DH}$; 10.–14. Answers will vary; 15. acute

Page 17

1. B, C, D, E, F, I; 2. A, G, H; Explanations will vary.

Page 18

Triangle–3; Quadrilateral–4; Pentagon–5; Hexagon–6; Octagon–8; 1. Triangle; 2. 4; 3. Pentagon; 4. 6; 5. 7; 6. Octagon; 7. 9; 8. 10; 9. E; 10. D; 11. B; 12. C; 13. A

Page 19

1. equilateral; 2. isosceles; 3. isosceles; 4. equilateral; 5. scalene; 6. isosceles; 7. scalene; 8. isosceles; 9. scalene

Page 20

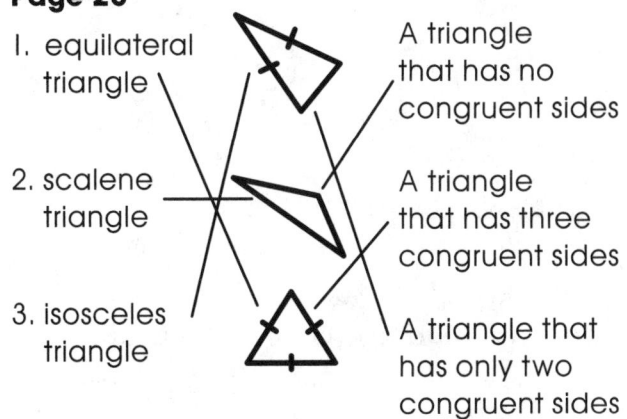

1. equilateral triangle — A triangle that has no congruent sides

2. scalene triangle — A triangle that has three congruent sides

3. isosceles triangle — A triangle that has only two congruent sides

4. isosceles
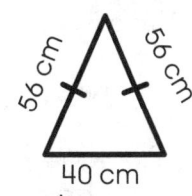
56 cm   56 cm   40 cm

5. equilateral

9 yd.   9 yd.   9 yd.

6. scalene
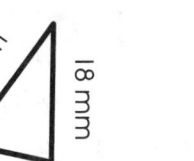
19 mm   18 mm   5 mm

7.

8.–9. Answers will vary

Page 21

1. acute; 2. right; 3. acute; 4. equiangular; 5. acute; 6. obtuse; 7. obtuse; 8. right; 9. equiangular

Page 22

1. D; 2. C; 3. A; 4. B; 5. B; 6. C; 7. T; 8. F; 9. T; 10. T; 11.–12. Answers will vary but should include that the sum of the angles of a triangle is 180°.

Page 23

1. right; 2. isosceles; 3. equilateral; 4. scalene; 5. obtuse; 6. equilateral; 7. scalene; 8. acute; 9. right; 10. isosceles; 11. scalene; 12. equiangular

Page 24

1. E; 2. A; 3. B; 4. G; 5. F; 6. D; 7. C; 8. sometimes; 9. never; 10. never; 11. A; 12. C

Page 25

1. 60°; 2. 50°; 3. 40°; 4. 68°; 5. 47°; 6. 38°; 7. 20°; 8. 54°

Page 26

1. 90°; 2. 30°; 3. 100°; 4. 20°; 5. 50°; 6. 63°; 7. 60°; 8. 55°; 9. 33°; 10. 43°; 11. 95°; 12. 6°

Page 27

1. square; 2. rhombus; 3. trapezoid; 4. square; 5. rectangle; 6. parallelogram; 7. rhombus; 8. trapezoid

Answer Key

Page 28

1. 100°; 2. 85°; 3. 90°; 4. 75°; 5. 100°; 6. 90°;
7. 102°; 8. 80°

Page 29

1. pentagon, I; 2. hexagon, R; 3. pentagon, I;
4. octagon, R; 5. hexagon, I; 6. pentagon, I

Page 30

Descriptions will vary. 1. hexagon;
2. parallelogram; 3. rectangle; 4. trapezoid;
5. octagon; 6. pentagon; 7. square; 8. triangle

Page 31

GEOMETRY IS FOR STARS.

Page 32

1. F; 2. B; 3. E; 4. A; 5. D; 6. H; 7. C; 8. J; 9. I;
10. G; 11.–16. Answers will vary

Page 33

1. $\overline{OM}$ or $\overline{LM}$ or $\overline{MN}$; 2. $\overline{LP}$ or $\overline{ON}$ or $\overline{LN}$; 3. $\overline{LN}$;
4. M; 5. Answers will vary but may include
$\overline{QR}$, $\overline{UR}$, $\overline{SR}$, $\overline{TR}$; 6. Answers will vary but may
include $\overline{UQ}$, $\overline{QT}$, $\overline{TS}$, $\overline{SU}$, $\overline{UT}$, $\overline{QS}$;
7. $\overline{UT}$ or $\overline{QS}$; 8. R

Page 34

1. 24 cm; 2. 124 ft.; 3. 24 km; 4. 18 cm;
5. 52 cm; 6. 168 in.; 7. 66 in.; 8. 224 ft.

Page 35

1. 8 cm; 2. 9 m; 3. 7 ft.; 4. 41 km; 5. 12 in.;
6. 3 ft.; 7. 45 cm; 8. 24 yd.

Page 36

1. 78 in.; 2. 18 cm; 3. 40 cm; 4. 28 mm; 5. 12 ft.;
6. 8 yd.; 7. 6 cm; 8. 3 ft.; 9. 11 yd.; 10. 5 in.;
11. 8 in.; 12. 2 cm

Page 37

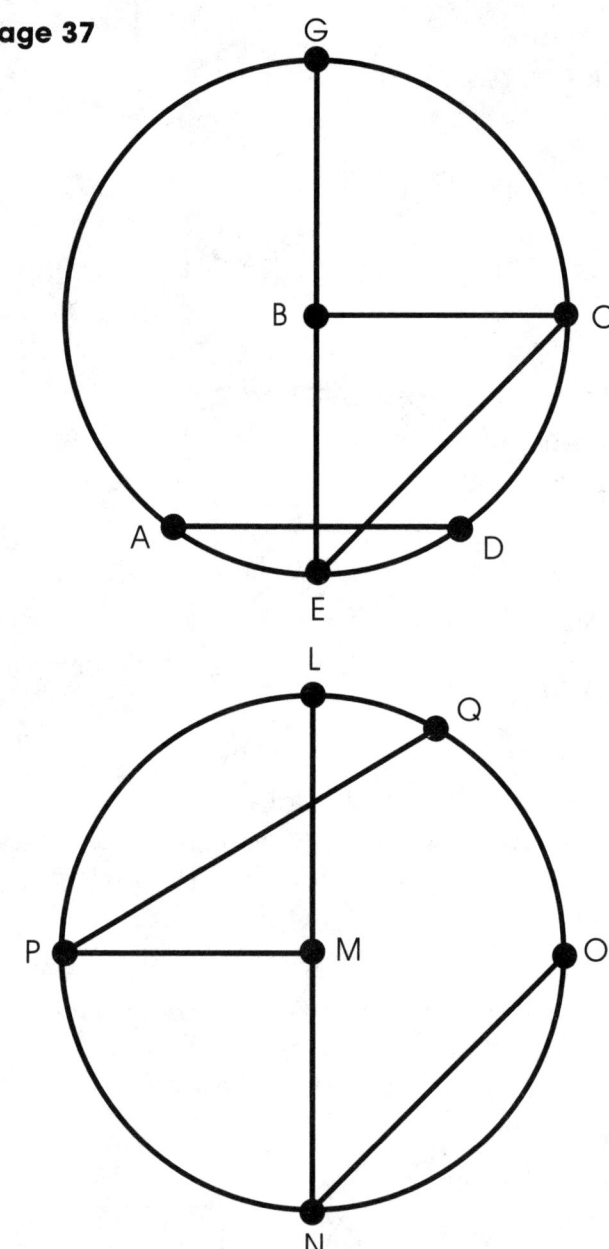

Page 38

1. radius $\overline{AB}$; 2. diameter $\overline{EF}$; 3. chord $\overline{IJ}$;
4. chord $\overline{KL}$; 5. center X; 6. chord $\overline{MN}$;
7. diameter $\overline{ST}$; 8. radius $\overline{XY}$; 9. diameter $\overline{GH}$;
10. center A; 11. chord $\overline{OP}$; 12. radius $\overline{QR}$;
13. radius $\overline{LM}$; 14. diameter $\overline{CD}$; 15. center N

Answer Key

Page 39

1.

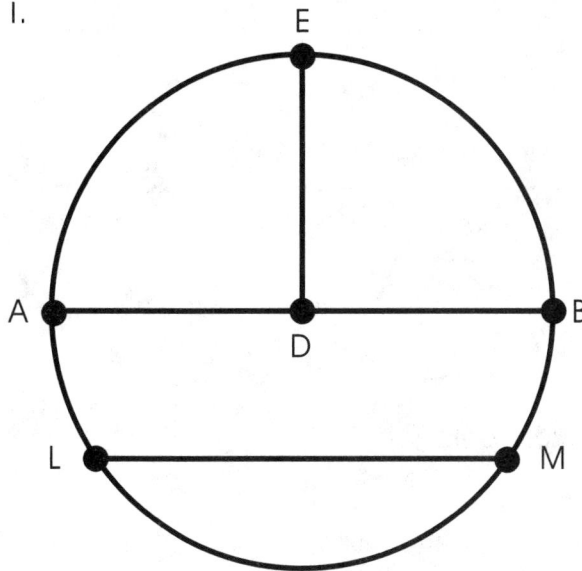

2.

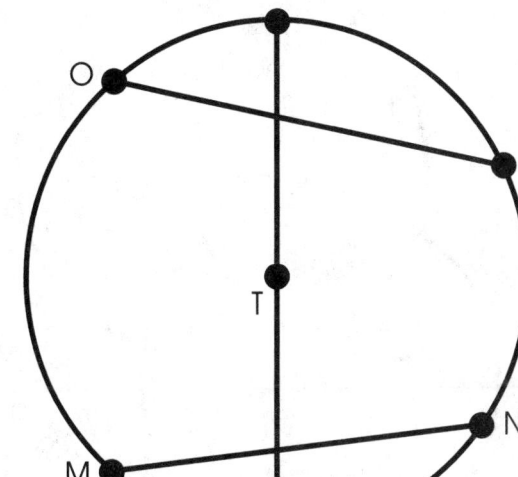

3.

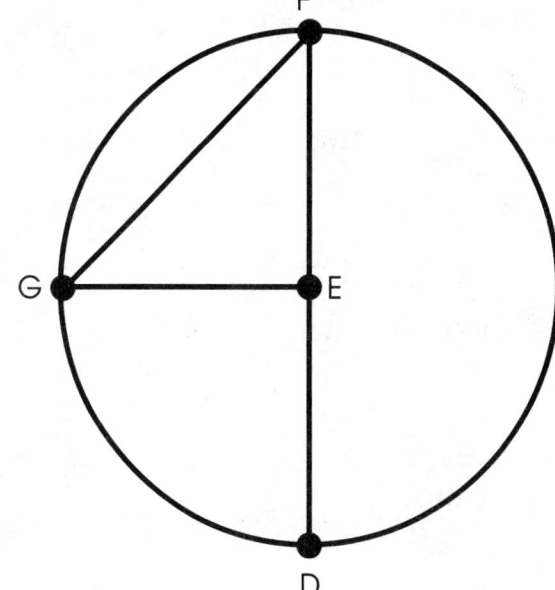

4.

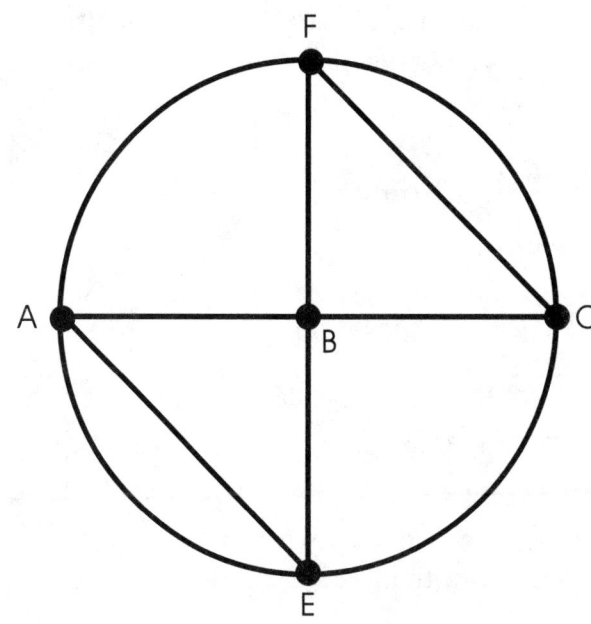

Page 40

1. two times the radius; 2. diameter divided by two; 3. diameter and/or chord; 4. diameter and/or chord; 5. radius; 6. center; 7. chord; 8.$\overline{MN}$

Answer Key

Page 41

Figure	Number of Faces	Number of Edges	Number of Vertices
Triangular Prism	5	9	6
Rectangular Prism	6	12	8
Triangular Pyramid	4	6	4
Cube	6	12	8
Square Pyramid	5	8	5

Page 42

1. prism; 2. pyramid; 3. prism; 4. cube;
5. prism; 6. prism; 7. cube; 8. pyramid

Page 43

1. cylinder; 2. sphere; 3. cone; 4. cylinder;
5. cone; 6. cone; 7. sphere; 8. cylinder

Page 44

1. square pyramid; 2. triangular prism;
3. rectangular prism

Page 45

Drawings will vary. 1. cylinder; 2. cube;
3. triangular prism; 4. rectangular prism;
5. sphere; 6. cone; 7. rectangular prism or
cube; 8. square pyramid; 9. triangular prism;
10. triangular pyramid

Page 46

Drawings will vary. 1. cube or rectangular
prism; 2. sphere; 3. cylinder; 4. rectangular
prism or cube; 5. cone; 6. triangular prism

Page 47

1.

2. circle, pentagon; 3. rectangle, square

Page 48

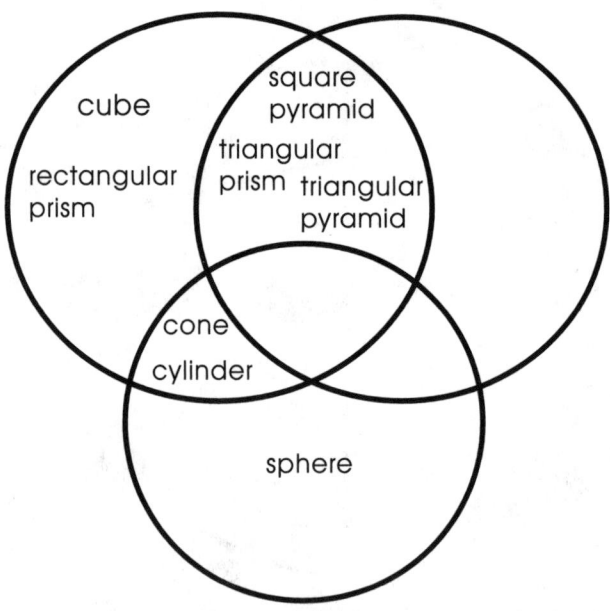

Answer Key

Page 49

Crossword grid answers:
1. PENTAGON
2. RECTANGLE
3. TRAPEZOID
4. VERTEX
5. SIDE
6. HEXAGON
7. FACE
8. OCTAGON
9. CYLINDER
10. CUBE
11. SQUARE
12. QUADRILATERAL
13. RECTANGULARPRISM
(PARALLELOGRAM, SPHERE)

Page 50

1. 50 yd.; 2. 21 in.; 3. 32 yd.; 4. 12 cm; 5. 40 in.;
6. 36 ft.; 7. 36 in.; 8. 14 cm; 9. 50 mm;
10. 49 mm; 11. 40 cm; 12. 46 in.

Page 51

1. 12 ft.; 2. 15 cm; 3. 6 yd.; 4. 2 in.; 5. 18 mm;
6. 6 ft.; 7. 22 cm; 8. 18 yd.; 9. 69 in.; 10. 40 ft.

Page 52

1. 12 yd.; 2. 18 ft.; 3. 48 ft.; 4. 26 in.; 5. 32 in.;
6. 42 mm; 7. 30 ft.; 8. 24 mm

Page 53

1. 200 ft.; 2. 240 ft.; 3. 760 ft.; 4. 24 ft.; 5. 112 ft.;
6. 60 in.; 7. 30 mm; 8. 63 ft.; 9. 20 ft.; 10. 40 ft.

Page 54

1. 18; 2. 11; 3. 10; 4. 17; 5. 12; 6. 8; 7. 8; 8. 13;
9. 10; 10. 13

Page 55

1. 30 square units; 2. 70 square units; 3. 36
square units; 4. 100 square units; 5. 117 square
units; 6. 42 square units; 7. 49 square units;
8. 32 square units; 9. 42 square units; 10. 26
square units; 11. 28 square units; 12. 36 square
units

Page 56

1. 81 ft.^{2}; 2. 40 in.^{2}; 3. 12 mm^2; 4. 168 cm^2;
5. 36 yd.^{2}; 6. 76 ft.^{2}; 7. 25 in.^{2}; 8. 60 cm^2;
9. 9 mm^2; 10. 4 ft.^{2}; 11. 91 m^2; 12. 100 km^2

Page 57

Rectangle	Width	Perimeter	Length	Area
A	1	6	**2**	2
B	2	**12**	4	8
C	3	18	6	**18**
D	4	24	**8**	32
E	5	30	10	**50**
F	6	**36**	12	72
G	7	42	**14**	98

1. rectangle G, yes; 2. as width goes up by
one, length goes up by two; 3. The area goes
up by four; 4. The perimeter doubles; 5. Yes.
Explanations will vary.

Page 58

Drawings will vary. 1. A = 6 units^2, P = Answers
will vary but must be greater than 12;
2. A = 6 units^2, P = Answers will vary but must
be greater than 12; 3. A = 6 units^2, P = Answers
will vary but must be less than 14; 4. A = 6
units^2, P = Answers will vary but must be less
than 14; 5.–7. Answers will vary.

Page 59

1. 60 cm^2; 2. 5 ft.^{2}; 3. 24 m^2; 4. 16 mm^2; 5. 70
in.^{2}; 6. 18 in.^{2}; 7. 24 m^2; 8. 54 in.^{2}; 9. 42 ft.^{2};
10. 20 ft.^{2}; 11. 32 cm^2; 12. 56 in.^{2}

Answer Key

Page 60

1. 150 ft.^{2}; 2. 14 cm^2; 3. 135 km^2; 4. 33 in.^{2};
5. 630 mm^2; 6. 25 in.^{2}; 7. 21 yd.^{2}; 8. 9 ft.^{2}

Page 61

Base	Height	Area
6 cm	2 cm	**6 cm^2**
8 cm	6 cm	**24 cm^2**
7 cm	2 cm	**7 cm^2**
8 cm	**14 cm**	56 cm^2
9 cm	4 cm	**18 cm^2**
10 cm	**14 cm**	70 cm^2
7 cm	6 cm	**21 cm^2**
12 cm	3 cm	18 cm^2
12 cm	9 cm	54 cm^2
10 cm	8 cm	**40 cm^2**
12 cm	**12 cm**	72 cm^2
18 cm	3 cm	27 cm^2
11 cm	4 cm	**22 cm^2**
24 cm	9 cm	108 cm^2
14 cm	4 cm	28 cm^2
10 cm	9 cm	**45 cm^2**
11 cm	6 cm	**33 cm^2**
9 cm	**16 cm**	72 cm^2
6 cm	**10 cm**	30 cm^2
22 cm	9 cm	99 cm^2
8 cm	**10 cm**	40 cm^2
12 cm	8 cm	**48 cm^2**
9 cm	6 cm	**27 cm^2**
5 cm	**14 cm**	35 cm^2
22 cm	8 cm	88 cm^2

Page 62

1. 60 yd.^{2}; 2. 55 m^2; 3. 30 ft.^{2}; 4. 39 cm^2;
5. 117 cm^2; 6. 75 ft.^{2}; 7. 96 in.^{2}; 8. 261 yd.^{2}

Page 63

1. 25 in.^{2}; 2. 36 mm^2; 3. 15 cm^2; 4.8 yd.^{2};
5. 12 in.^{2}; 6. 8 ft.^{2}; 7. 18 cm^2; 8. 32 mm^2

Page 64

1. 7 yd.; 2. 4 in.; 3. 36 m^2; 4. 18 ft.^{2}; 5. 45 m^2;
6. 8 in.

Page 65

1. 30 cm; 2. 150 m^2; 3. 96 in.; 4. 30 cm^2;
5. 12 in.; 6. 88 m

Page 66

1. 7; 2. 15; 3. 10; 4. 11; 5. 20; 6. 13; 7. 15 cubic
units; 8. 6 cubic units; 9. 6 cubic units

Page 67

1. 24 in.^{3}; 2. 72 cm^3; 3. 96 yd.^{3}; 4. 90 ft.^{3};
5. 180 mm^3; 6. 20 in.^{3}; 7. 38 in.^{3}; 8. 245 cm^3

Page 68

Length	Width	Height	Volume
2 mm	4 mm	6 mm	48 mm^3
8 mm	5 mm	1 mm	**40 mm^3**
2 mm	9 mm	4 mm	**72 mm^3**
3 mm	3 mm	18 mm	162 mm^3
12 mm	2 mm	**3 mm**	72 mm^3
31 mm	3 mm	3 mm	279 mm^3
2 mm	11 mm	4 mm	**88 mm^3**
6 mm	9 mm	**2 mm**	108 mm^3
5 mm	4 mm	8 mm	**160 mm^3**
15 mm	**6 mm**	3 mm	270 mm^3
12 mm	3 mm	3 mm	**108 mm^3**
23 mm	3 mm	**1 mm**	69 mm^3
10 mm	5 mm	11 mm	550 mm^3
9 mm	**3 mm**	20 mm	540 mm^3
2 mm	14 mm	6 mm	**168 mm^3**
4 mm	1 mm	15 mm	60 mm^3

Page 69

1. C; 2. A; 3. D; 4. A; 5. B; 6. D

Page 70

Circumference measurements (C) are
approximations.

Answer Key

Circle #	C	d	C ÷ d
1	15 cm	4.7 cm	3.19
2	11 cm	3.5 cm	3.14
3	13 cm	4 cm	3.25
4	8 cm	2.5 cm	3.2
5	14 cm	4.5 cm	3.11

Page 71

1. 50.24 in.; 2. 113.04 in.; 3. 59.66 cm;
4. 50.24 ft.; 5. 69.08 cm; 6. 31.4 m; 7. 34.54 cm;
8. 87.92 in.

Page 72

1. 69.08 cm; 2. 25.12 mm; 3. 56.52 ft.;
4. 50.24 mm; 5. 50.24 in.; 6. 62.8 cm;
7. 69.08 yd.; 8. 56.52 in.; 9. 97.34 yd.;
10. 18.84 in.; 11. 18.84 ft.; 12. 75.36 ft.;
13. 106.76 cm; 14. 37.68 ft.; 15. 28.26 in.;
16. 12.56 yd.; 17. 100.48 mm; 18. 37.68 cm;
19. 109.9 ft.; 20. 596.6 in.; 21. 25.12 yd.

Page 73

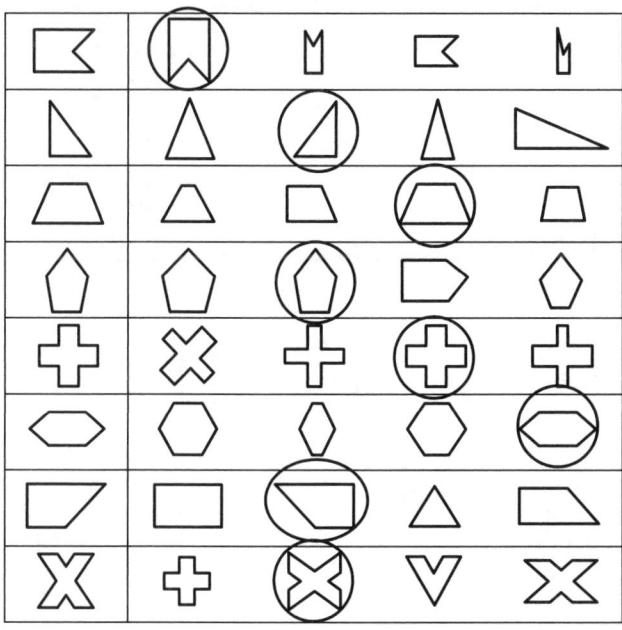

Page 74

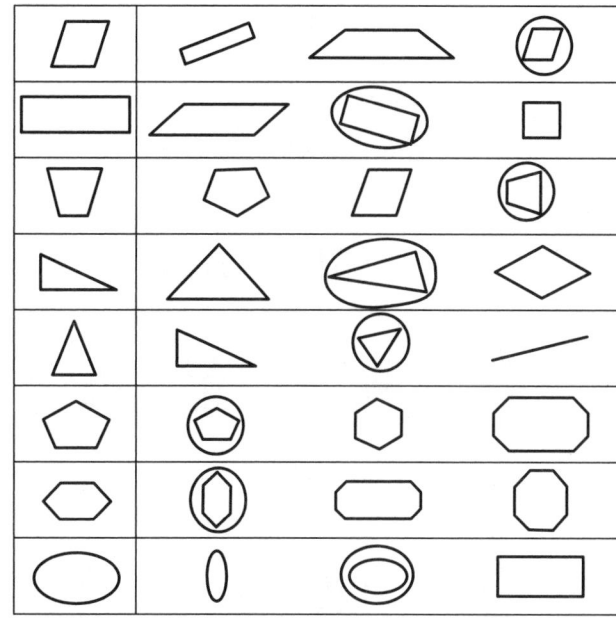

Page 75

1. congruent; 2. congruent; 3. similar;
4. similar; 5. congruent; 6. similar; 7. similar;
8. congruent; 9. similar; 10. congruent;
11. congruent; 12. similar; 13. congruent;
14. congruent; 15. congruent

Page 76

1. 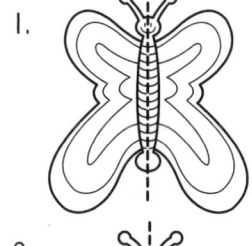 2.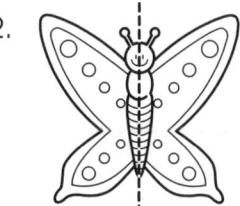

3.  4.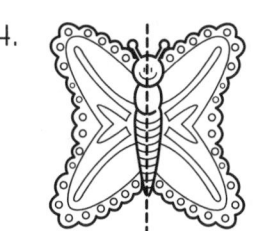

5. 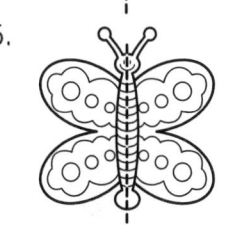 6.

7. Answers will vary

Answer Key

Page 77

1. yes
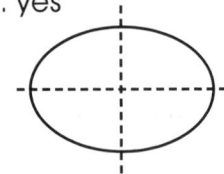

2. yes

3. yes
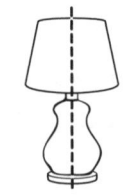

4. yes
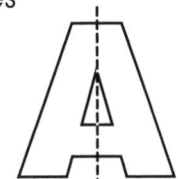

5. yes

6. yes
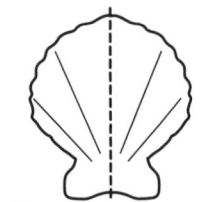

7. no

8. yes
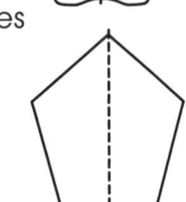

9. no

10. Answers will vary

Page 78

Answers will vary

Page 79

1.
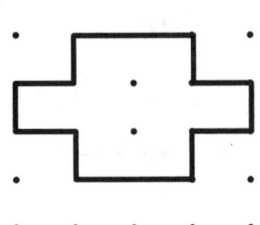

2.

3.
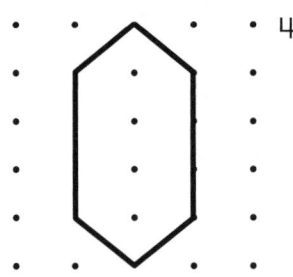

4.
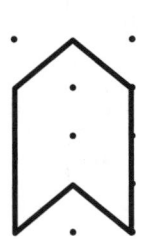

5.
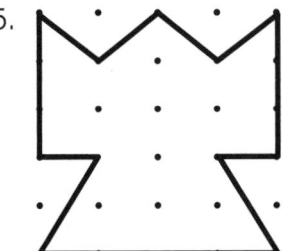

6.

7.
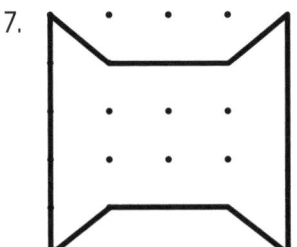

8.
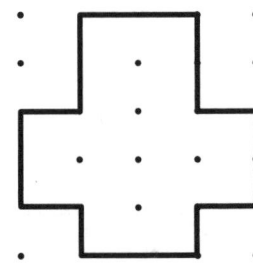

9.
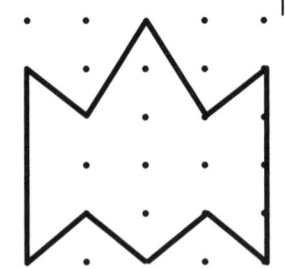

10.

11.
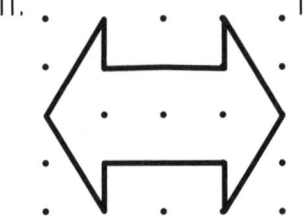

12.

Answer Key

13.

14.

15.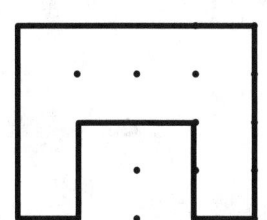

Page 80

Answers will vary

Page 81

1.

2.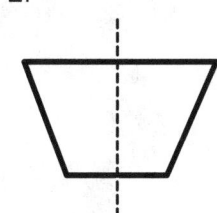

3.

4.

5.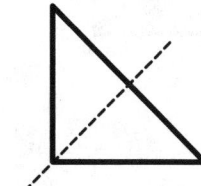

6.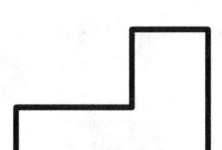

7.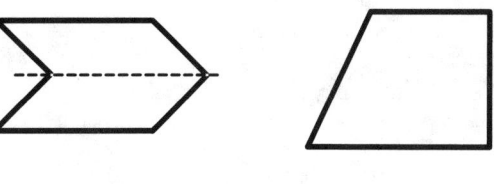

8.

9.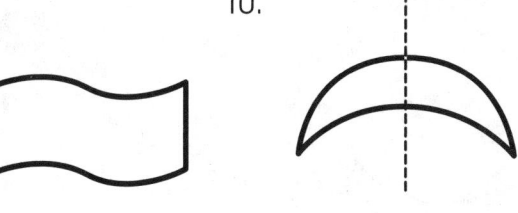

10.

11.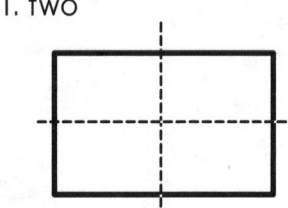

12.

Page 82

1. two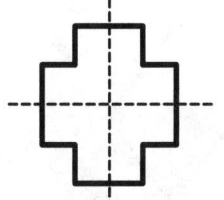

2. two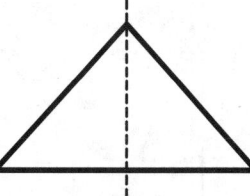

3. two

4. one

Answer Key

5. one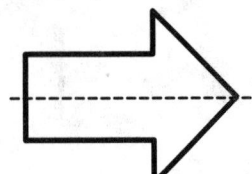

6. two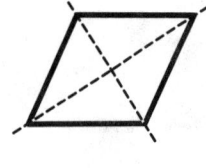

3. one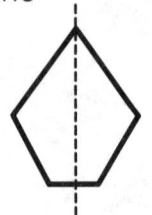

4. none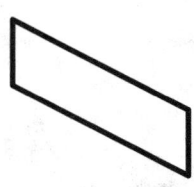

7. two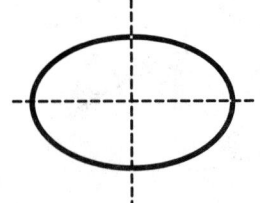

8. two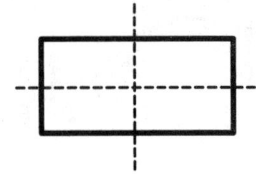

5. eight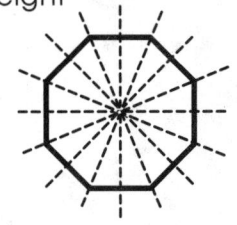

6. one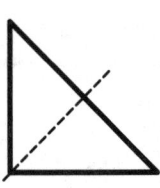

9. two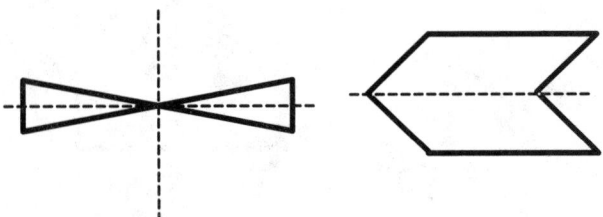

10. one

7. one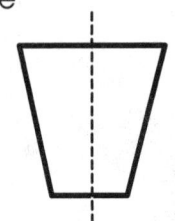

8. one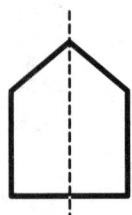

11. none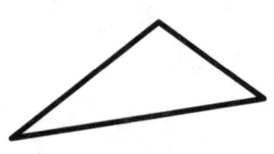

12. one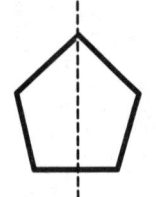

9. two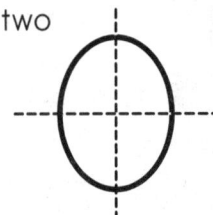

10. two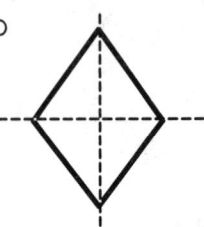

11. one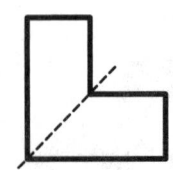

12. four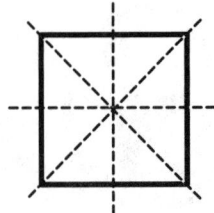

Page 83

1. one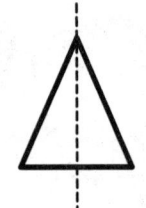

2. two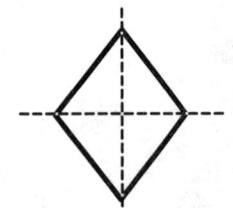

13. five

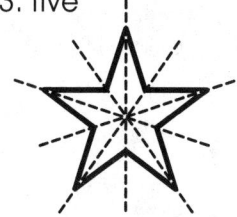

14. one

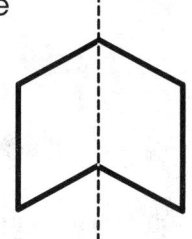

5.

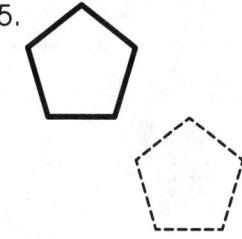

6.

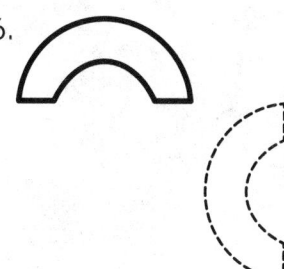

15. none

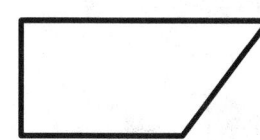

7.

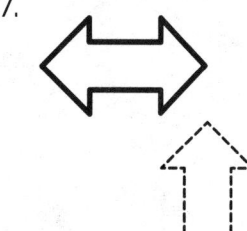

8.

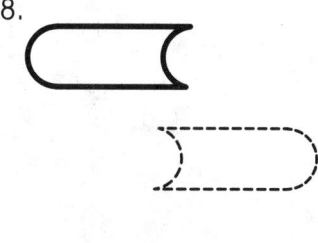

Page 84

1. turn; 2. flip; 3. turn; 4. slide; 5. turn; 6. flip;
7. slide; 8. turn; 9. turn; 10. turn; 11. slide; 12.
flip; 13. turn; 14. slide; 15. turn; 16. slide

Page 85

1. slide; 2. slide; 3. flip; 4. turn; 5. none; 6. flip;
7. turn; 8. none

9.

10.

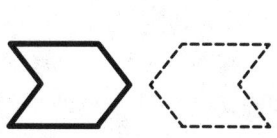

Page 86

1.

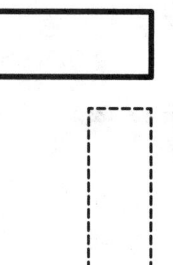

2.

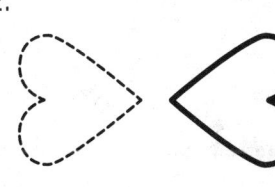

11.

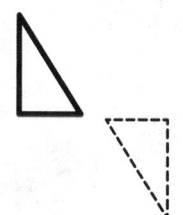

12.

3.

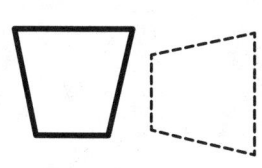

4.

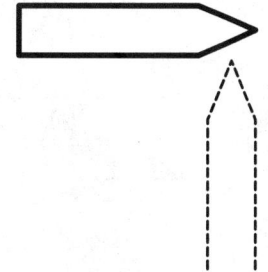

Page 87

1. slide; 2. flip; 3. 90° or 270° turn; 4. 90° turn;
5. 90° or 270° turn; 6. flip or 90° turn

7.

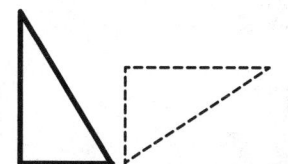

8.

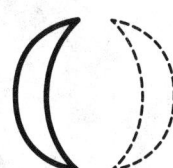

9. 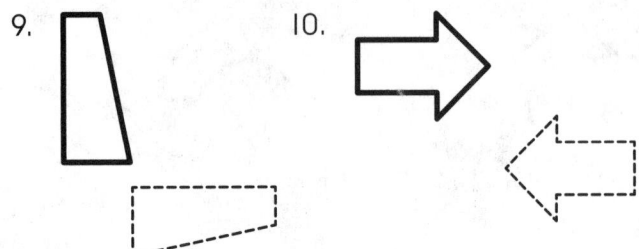 10.

11. 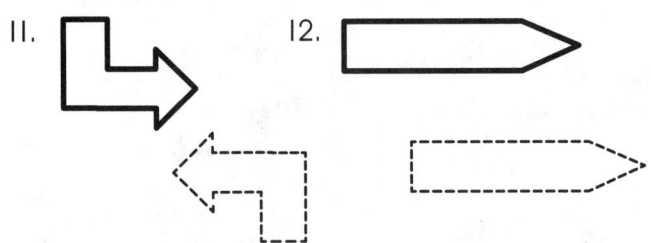 12.

Page 88

1. They are similar but not congruent;
2. Answers will vary; 3. Figures must be the same size and shape to be congruent;
4. No, because similar figures are the same shape; 5. No, because congruent figures are the same size and shape; 6. Yes, because similar figures are the same shape; 7. B;
8. D

Page 89

1. A; 2. B.; 3. A. slide, B. flip, C. turn;
4. A. 2   B. 0   C. 2

 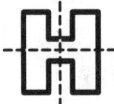

5. A. 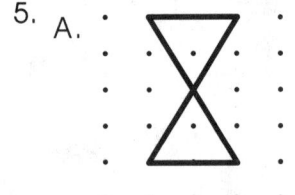   B.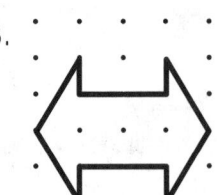

C.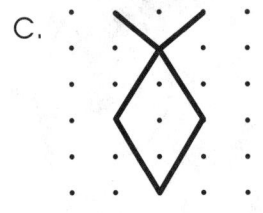

Page 90

1. yes; 2. no; 3. yes; 4. and 5. Answers will vary.

Page 91

1.–7. Answers will vary; 8. an arrangement of plane figures that covers a surface without overlapping or leaving any gaps

Page 92

1.–6.

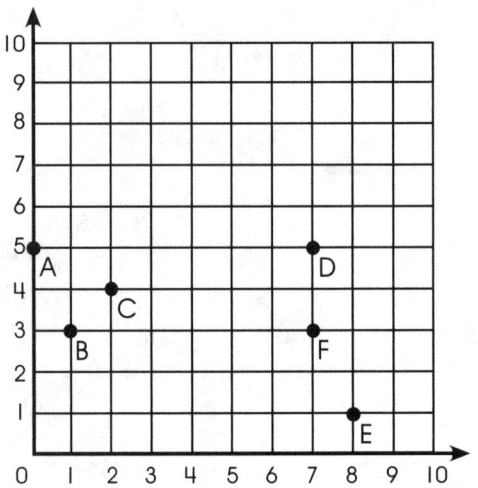

7. (2, 3); 8 (4, 9); 9. (5, 1); 10. (7, 7); 11. (8, 4); 12. (9, 2)

Page 93

1. rhombus

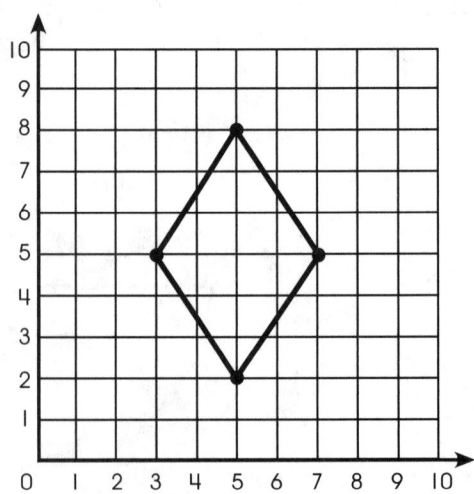

Answer Key

2. and 3. irregular hexagon

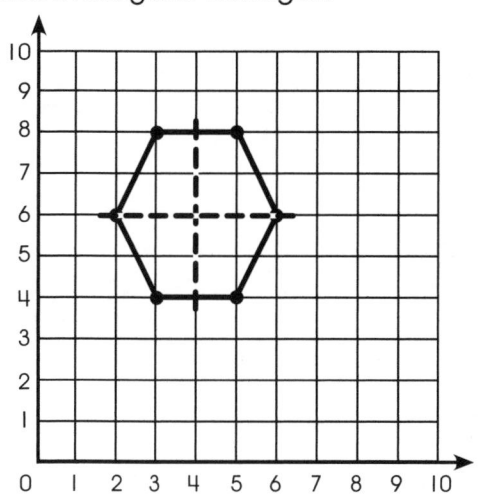

Page 94

1. (8, 8); 2. (2, 7); 3. 8

4.

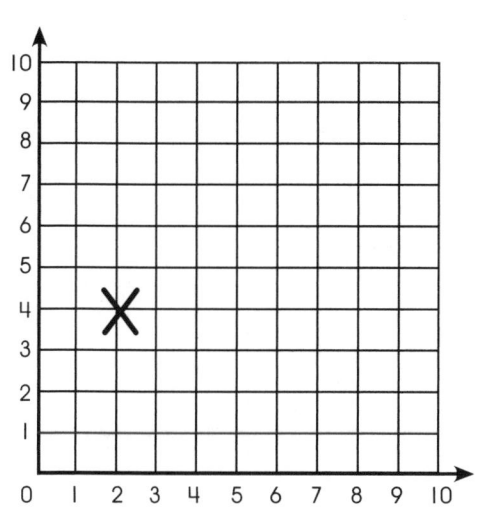

5. 10

Page 95

1. (4, 10); 2. (9, 9); 3. (8, 6); 4. (5, 5); 5. (3, 3);
6. (5, 1); 7. (2, 8); 8. (7, 8); 9. (5, 3); 10. (1, 5);
11. (2, 1,); 12. (7, 3); 13 (3, 5); 14 (8, 1)

Page 96

1. Remote Control Car; 2. Robot; 3. Board
Game; 4. Puzzle; 5. Soccer Ball; 6. Paintbrush;
7. Markers; 8. Chemistry Set; 9. Baseball Bat;
10. Monkey; 11. Video Game; 12. Bicycle

Page 97

A "PLANE" CHEESEBURGER

Page 98

1. house

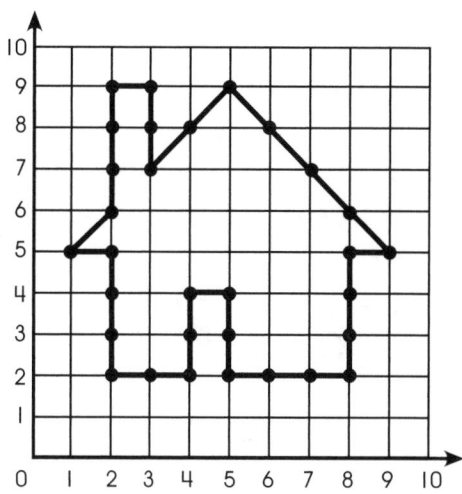

Page 99

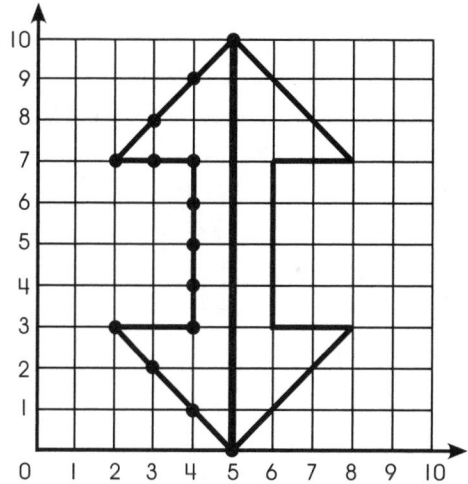

Page 100

1. (2, 9); 2. (3, 8); 3. (9, 8); 4. (6, 5); 5. (5, 2);
6. (8, 1)

7.–12.

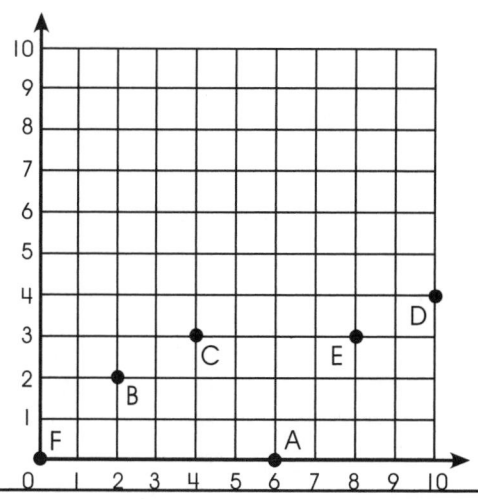

Answer Key

Page 101

1.–6.

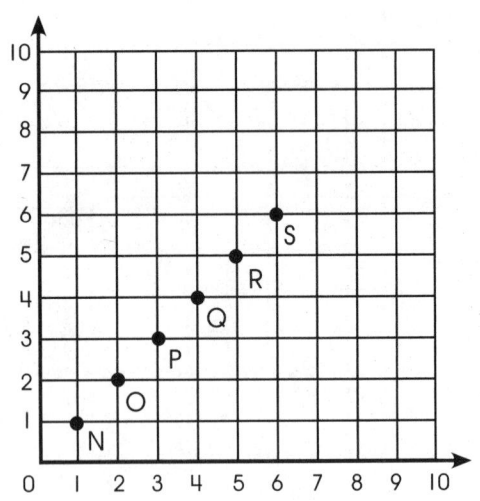

7. (1, 9); 8. (3, 7); 9. (5, 5); 10. (7, 3); 11. (9, 1);
12. (10, 10)

Page 102

1. (1, 8); 2. (2, 6); 3. (3, 4); 4. (4, 5); 5. (5, 6);
6. (6, 7)

7.–12.

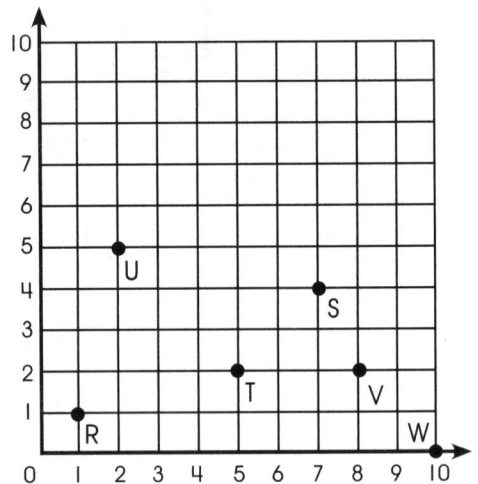

Final Review

Page 103

1. B; 2. A; 3. right; 4.–9. Answers
will vary.

Page 104

10. A; 11. C; 12. F; 13. B;
14. C; 15. right triangle; 16. irregular pentagon;
17. square or rectangle

Page 105

18. 360; 19. pi; 20. width; 21. 180;
22. coordinate; 23. right; 24. perimeter;
25. height; 26. angles; 27. cube; 28. cylinder;
29. sphere; 30. 8 cm; 31. 52 in.; 32. 59.66 ft.

Page 106

33. Yes. Explanations will vary; 34. They are
the same size; 35. C; 36. false; 37. B; 38.
scalene triangle; 39. No, because the total of
all three angles equals 180°; 40. B;
41. C

Page 107

42. turn; 43. flip; 44. slide; 45. 8; 46. B; 47. A;
48. B

Page 108

49. A = 60 yd.^{2}, P = 34 yd.; 50. A = 76 ft.^{2},
P = 46 ft.; 51. A = 150 ft.^{2}, P = 71 ft.; 52. 7 cube
units; 53. 245 cm^3; 54. 72 cm^3

55.–60.

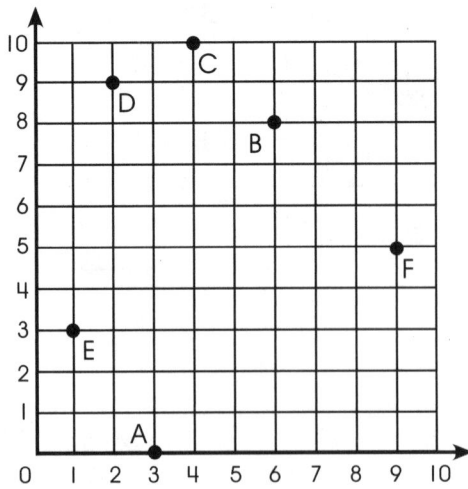